FROM HATE TO LOVE

A SPIRITUAL JOURNEY TO HEAL

FRANK J. DONOHUE

The principles outlined in Frank J Donohue's From Hate to Love will not only speak to your soul, but they will give aid and solace to your mental, physical, and spiritual health. The author has a special insight into the world based on his experiences, and I highly recommend you take the time to explore the wonderful offerings of **From Hate to Love**.

—Mark Graham, author of The Harbinger, The Missing Sixth, and The Fire Theft.

This is a really great inspirational book for the times we are facing. It opens your eyes and reminds us all we can choose to love our neighbor, but we have to start by loving ourselves. It's very well written. I'm going to read this more than once and give it / recommend it for the people I care about.

—Melanie Churella Johnson, #1 Best Selling Author

Who better to offer a big-picture view of life than a veteran pilot? Readjust your perspective and read **From Hate to Love**. *You'll be glad you did.*

—Mark Stevens, Author of the Allison Coil Mystery Series, Colorado Book Award and Authors league Award 2016.

Escape the hate! Frank J Donohue's **From Hate to Love** *will help set your soul free, and experience the healing power of love today! For nearly four decades, he piloted aircraft through the heavens. And like all of us, he's had his share of ups and downs, sunny days and cloudy skies. Now, Frank draws on those incredible experiences, including his and his wife's near-death experiences to encourage us to confront fear and hatred. This book has helped me to first to not hate, then to like and then to work to love others. I am recommending this book to my friends.*

—Jamie J Warren, #1 New York Times Bestreader

From Hate to Love: A Spiritual Journey to Heal

Copyright © 2020 Frank J. Donohue

Published by NOT-Y, Virginia Beach, VA

ISBN 978-0-9894678-6-5 (Print)
ISBN 978-0-9894678-7-2 (eBook)

Library of Congress Control Number: 2020916316

Cover and Book Design by ebooklaunch.com

Unless otherwise noted, Scripture texts in this work are taken from the New American Bible, revised edition© 2010, 1991, 1986, 1970 Confraternity of Christian Doctrine, Washington, D.C. and are used by permission of the copyright owner. All Rights Reserved. No part of the New American Bible may be reproduced in any form without permission in writing from the copyright owner.

Scripture texts marked NIV taken from the Holy Bible, New International Version®, NIV®. Copyright © 1973, 1978, 1984, 2011 by Biblica, Inc.™ Used by permission of Zondervan. All rights reserved worldwide. www.zondervan.com The "NIV" and "New International Version" are trademarks registered in the United States Patent and Trademark Office by Biblica, Inc.™

All rights reserved. No part of this publication may be reproduced or transmitted in any form or by any means, mechanical or electronic, including photocopying and recording, or by any information storage and retrieval system, without permission in writing from author or publisher (except by a reviewer, who may quote brief passages and/or show brief video clips in a review).

Although the author and publisher have made every effort to ensure that the information in this book was correct at press time, the author and publisher do not assume and hereby disclaim any liability to any party for any loss, damage, or disruption caused by errors or omissions, whether such errors or omissions result from negligence, accident, or any other cause.

First Edition Printed in the United States of America

I dedicate this book to Francis and Jared and to all the people who still have a chance to avoid the fires of hell.

https://frankjdonohue.com/tenhealthytips

TABLE OF CONTENTS

Foreword i
Introduction 1
CHAPTER ONE: Help Me 5
CHAPTER TWO: *"Save us from the fires of hell"* 9
CHAPTER THREE: How Did We Get Here? 14
CHAPTER FOUR: What People Believe 19
CHAPTER FIVE: Pray to Not Hate 33
CHAPTER SIX: "Trinity for Me" Dissected 40
CHAPTER SEVEN: Jesus Taught Us 50
CHAPTER EIGHT: Why We Hate 53
CHAPTER NINE: Not Hate for Health 60
CHAPTER TEN: How to Not Hate 63
CHAPTER ELEVEN: Start Now to Not Hate 74
Acknowledgments 79
Appendix 80
Bibliography 81
Notes 84
About the Author 87

Foreword

In From Hate to Love: A Spiritual Journey to Heal, *Frank Donohue helps us to set a course for a good life—a good life that respects and loves all other human beings, which will hopefully allow us to live in eternal joy with our Creator, our God.*

I have had the pleasure of becoming friends with Frank through a number of volunteer activities at our church, the Church of the Holy Family, in Virginia Beach. We have spent most of our time together sharing our faith with the youth of our parish in weekly educational and discussion groups. As he states in his book, we frequently learn as much about ourselves and our faith from them as they learn from us.

Most of my good friends come from parish life, as they share the same principles of living as I do. Frank is one of those people. I have learned of his strong faith in God and humanity. He has a strong desire to share his knowledge and prescription for a proper life as evidenced by the book you are holding. He wants to help you become the best person you can be.

As a family physician, I have learned about, and witnessed in my practice, the physiologic effects of a life lived with love for others. A life without hate. The principles outlined in From Hate to Love *will not only help your soul, but will help your mental and physical health while you live your human existence. Your journey will be healthier and happier.*

Frank shares personal details of how his guiding principles have helped his life and I am grateful that he is sharing them with us. He realizes we are all struggling in a world that seems to make it easier to hate, but he truly wants us all to overcome that and live a more positive, meaningful life. He will be happy if one person's life will be transformed by his words, but I think there will be many. Thank you, Frank.

—Ted Kubicki, MD

INTRODUCTION

There is too much hate today, and it is making people sick. Too much hate exists in the newspaper, on the radio, on television, on social media, and in our social groups. There are over a thousand hate groups in the United States today. People are taking this hate to church, to school, to work, to social media and to their homes. There are family members who have stopped talking to each other because of hate of the other person's political affiliation.

There is a phenomenal increase in partisan divide driven by hate of the other side. Those who are different become enemies and should be hated; many people of influence promote this. Hate is becoming more normal and more socially acceptable.

This must stop! After all, the genetic DNA makeup of all humans on planet earth is 99.9 percent identical. We humans have more in common with each other than that which divides us. We must join together and transform ourselves from not hating to loving. I wrote this book to change people's hearts from hating to loving.

This book touches briefly on the subject matters of the origins of planet Earth and human beings and maintains that some super nonhuman being was involved in the process. A creator or a god may exist and does not want us to hate. It gives a brief history of some of the most popular religions of the world and how most of these religions teach not to hate. Many historical prophets provide prayers indicating not to hate.

Pray prayers to help yourself to not hate. Some of these prayers are provided, as well as a special bonus prayer that I wrote that might help you. This bonus prayer can be customized and changed according to your situational needs and places of gratitude. There is an explanation of the spiritual influences on this prayer and how its words were written.

This book attempts to answer some of the following questions: Who was the ultimate example of how to forgive and not hate? Who are we? Why were we created? Why are we here? What is our purpose in this life? Are we here to just suck everything we can out of people and out of Earth's resources? Or should we give back to the people and planet Earth?

Should we pray for people? Should we make sacrifices for people? Should we help and love people? Should we like people? Should we hate people? Why do people hate other people and what are some of the ways you can learn not to hate? What are the health advantages and disadvantages of hating and of not hating?

If just one answer, tip or suggestion from this book influences just one person in some way Not to Hate one person, then I will be happily rewarded, and my revised lifelong goal to help mankind will have been achieved. You don't have to be old to not hate and you don't have to be an adult to not hate. **No matter where you are and where you have been, you can start not hating.** Everyone is capable of not hating.

Note: In my previous career I aviated jet airplanes around the world for over thirty years, so it is unavoidable that I have let personal stories seep into my writings.

To hate a person can be really bad for your health. To love a person can be really good for your health. Hating can make you sick; it can make you sick mentally, physically and spiritually. If for no other reason you need to read *From Hate to Love: A Spiritual Journey to Heal* because of the health consequences that could affect your well-being and even your longevity.

CHAPTER ONE

HELP ME

Help me, the virus is making me sick. The COVID-19 virus can make you really sick. According to CDC.gov, people who contract the COVID-19 virus may have the following systems: fever or chills, cough, shortness of breath or difficulty breathing, fatigue, muscle or body aches, headache, new loss of taste or smell, sore throat, congestion or runny nose, nausea or vomiting, and/or diarrhea. You should seek emergency medical care immediately if you have these warning signs: trouble breathing, persistent pain or pressure in the chest, new confusion, inability to wake or stay awake and or bluish lips or face.

Help me, hating is making me sick. Hating can make you sick, real sick; physically, mentally and spiritually. Hate is like poison, like emotional poison tearing up your inside and causing health destruction. Hating can cause anxiety, loss of valuable sleep, depression, headaches, upset stomach and many more ailments. Hating can break down your nervous system, immune system, and endocrine system and destroy your mental well-being. Hate can destroy you emotionally and make your body more vulnerable to sickness and disease by compromising your immune system. Hating creates a destructive state of mind that can be detrimental to your physical health and your emotional and spiritual well-being.

Hatred is a feeling that everyone has felt and experienced at some point in our lives. Although hate can be directed toward anything like jobs, chores, ideas, food, animals, places, et cetera, it is the hate toward other people that is the most destructive. Hate is very hurtful, especially when we feel we've been betrayed or hurt by someone for whom we have good, strong feelings. When one feels that they have been seriously wronged or victimized by someone, then one feels the need to blame that person for one's own unhappiness and anger, and hatred starts to develop.

The effects of hatred over a long period of time can be devastating to your physical, mental and spiritual health. Hate can poison your soul and damage other relationships in your life. Unlike the COVID-19 virus, for which we will eventually invent a vaccine, there is no vaccine to fight hate. We will have to undergo physical, mental and spiritual therapy to overcome the hate in our lives and transform it in the direction of love. This will not be easy, but it can be done.

If you have ever been the person who has been hated, then you are aware that the overall effects of being hated can be physically harmful and emotionally devastating. You feel upset and frightened, and your self-esteem descends to an all-time low. You may lose sleep, eat unhealthily, and/or put dangerous substances or fluids into your precious human body.

If you have experienced how it feels when you're hated, imagine how it feels to the other person when you hate them. Do you really want that on your conscience? Do you want that on your soul? How will you face Jesus on that day He judges you and you have to explain why you hated a person He loved? Remember, Jesus loves everyone; yes, Jesus loves you and me.

Don't feed hatred and promote its destructive growth. Confront hatred, understand hatred, undergo therapy and transform it so you do not hate, and you are able to promote your constructive personal growth. Only you have the choice to hold on to hatred where the emotion will make you sicker, or the choice to embrace kindness and love where the emotions will help you heal. The sooner you get rid of this toxic emotion of hating, the less damage it will do to you and the healthier and happier you will be. These are the steps throughout this book that we will study to help transform us from hating to loving:

1) We will examine proofs that God and Jesus exist. Why do we exist? Do you believe you are here just to suck everything out of life for your own happiness? Or should you love other people and try not to hate anyone?
2) We will discover what other people believe. Every religion is similar to some or all religions, and every religion is different from some or all religions. Through a synopsis of the world's most widespread religions we will discover what most religions teach about hate.
3) We will read a special prayer I wrote to help you not hate. Numerous religious prophets gave us prayers to help us not to hate. I believe the Holy Spirit influenced me to write this special prayer to help people not to hate, and instead transition to love. The words of this prayer are based on Scriptures from the Holy Bible, a source of the teachings of Jesus. Jesus taught us how to not hate, and He is the perfect example of how to not hate, but instead to forgive and to love. We will ask God the Father, the Holy Spirit, and Jesus to help us. We will also ask Jesus's mother, Mary, to

help us. Included is a grace blessing to Mary to interject with Jesus to help not hate.
4) We will dig further into some of the reasons people hate and the health consequences of hating. Several recommendations on how not to hate are examined. There is an expanded version of one technique that could help you transform from merely not hating, to loving.
5) Near the end I will present some of the things I am doing to not hate, in order to love and to give back.
6) We'll finish up with a call to action to start not to hate and to start to love all people. If for no other reason, start to not hate and instead start to love for your own health benefits and well-being. Your longevity may depend on it. Reading this book will help you.

Notice the title of the book, *From Hate to Love*. Throughout this book, the phrase "I Will Not Hate You" is interjected numerous times to remind you and me not to hate. Associate the phrase "I Will Not Hate You" with the title *From Hate to Love*. Whenever you are confronted with a person or situation that is tempting you to hate or dislike, say to yourself, **"I Will Not Hate You."** Saying "I Will Not Hate You" will trigger your memory to recall parts of this book that will help you.

First, I want to start out with what scared me the most to not hate any person and increase my capacity to love all people. As a pilot captain of jet airplanes with thirty-six years of flight experience, flight emergences have not scared me. Do you want to know what scares me? Death and the fires of hell scare me!

CHAPTER TWO

"SAVE US FROM THE FIRES OF HELL"

"She opened Her hands once more, as She had done the two previous months. The rays [of light] appeared to penetrate the earth, and we saw, as it were, a vast sea of fire. Plunged in this fire, we saw the demons and the souls [of the damned]. The latter were like transparent burning embers, all blackened or burnished bronze, having human forms. They were floating about in that conflagration, now raised into the air by the flames, which issued from within themselves, together with great clouds of smoke. Now they fell back on every side like sparks in huge fires, without weight or equilibrium, amid shrieks and groans of pain and despair, which horrified us and made us tremble with fright (it must have been this sight which caused me to cry out, as people say they heard me). The demons were distinguished [from the souls of the damned] by their terrifying and repellent likeness to frightful and unknown animals, black and transparent like burning coals. That vision only lasted for a moment, thanks to our good Heavenly Mother, who at the first apparition had promised to take us to Heaven. Without that, I think that we would have died of terror and fear."[1]

Imagine you're looking up at a beautiful lady, Holy Mary, Mother of Jesus Christ, and she's giving you a vision of what hell is. She projects rays of light that seems to penetrate the Earth's surface to give you a vivid vision of hell. In this vision there is a sea of fire burning hot with flashy sunlike fiery flames. You see humanlike life forms and nonhumanlike life forms floating above a sea of ferocious fire.

The life forms descend and touch the electrifying fire—sparks ignite. Then those life forms rise up with flames from within them that form gloomy gray clouds of smoke. These humanlike figures become blackened and transparent like burning coals. These poor souls encounter great pain and are crying out for help.

Have you ever touched a hot surface and burned your finger or hand? At age 26, while I was in flight school, a car radiator cap exploded and burned my whole right arm. The hot radiator fluid burnt almost four of the seven layers of skin off my arm. The skin is the largest organ of the body. I was in the hospital for over a week, and it took months for my skin to heal. I experienced a lot of pain.

Now, imagine these human souls floating up and down, touching the hot sea of explosive flames and rising up with burned and blackened scars all over their bodies. The vision given to the children at Fatima was so frightful that it almost scared them to death. It was only the promise from Holy Mother Mary that the three children would go to heaven that kept the children from being scared to death by the frightful visions of terrible hell. I reflected for several hours, then for several days, and eventually for several months on the possibility that these children experienced the true vision of what hell is like.

In her *Memoirs*, Sister Lucy of Fatima, Portugal, describes the vision of hell, a secret that the Holy Blessed Virgin Mary, Mother of Jesus Christ, revealed to Lucy Santos and Jacinta and Francisco Marto in 1917. At Fatima, Mary also revealed to the children a second secret that

World War I would end and a third secret of the failed assassination attempt of Pope John Paul II. The second and third secret revelations came true, so I assume the first secret also must be true.

The last apparition in Fatima occurred on October 13, 1217, to over 70,000 people who experienced the appearance of the sun zigzagging in motion with brilliant radiant dancing rays known as the "Sun Miracle."[2] Other ghostlike images of Mary have been revealed to humans on more than 300 occasions worldwide. Marian apparitions have occurred in Portugal, France, Ireland, Belgium, Poland, Italy, Mexico, Egypt, Africa and many other places. At Fatima, the Blessed Virgin Mary told the three children that many souls would go to hell because they have no one to pray or make sacrifices for them.

It is amazing how the conscience and the brain operate at times. Months after I read Sister Lucy's memoirs, I was pondering death and the possibility that these children experienced the true vision of what hell is like. There were several times I believe I almost died. My parents told me that at age two I almost fell out of a car while traveling at sixty miles per hour on the Long Island Expressway. At age 13, some hoodlums pointed a loaded gun at our small group and particularly me on Halloween night while we were trick-or-treating. At 17, while driving on New York Highway 17 during a severe snowstorm, I almost did not recover from a 360-degree skid next to a gorge.

At 21, I was a passenger in an auto accident while en route from Madrid to Benidorm, Spain; I almost did not survive. Six months later, while driving in the English Midland Mountains en route to Glasgow, Scotland, I barely survived an auto spinout on black ice. At age 22, I was rescued during an auto breakdown located in one of the worst brush fires in Nevada. At age 27, I survived a near-drowning incident in the ocean off Bondi Beach in Sydney, Australia. At age 28, while in a hotel room in Frankfurt, Germany, I had a choking incident and passed out; I survived.

At age 54, I helped resuscitate a man having a heart attack in Cabo Roig, Spain. Six months later, I was presented with the ultimate test: I resuscitated my wife during the initial stage of a tragic ruptured brain aneurysm at our home. There were several flight situations during my aviation career that could have ended in death. Of all the death experiences I encountered, it was this last experience of seeing my wife close her eyes and stop breathing that stunned me into really appreciating life.

I learned to be totally grateful for every moment of life, because life is precious, valuable, delicate and unpredictable. Enjoy the day, if not the night, and pray, "Thank you for this moment of life," because you do not know when your last moment of life will be.

We know what happens when we are born, but what happens when we die? No one really knows what happens when we die. Who are we? Why were we created? Why are we here? What is our purpose in this life?

Are we here to just suck everything we can out of people and out of Earth's resources? Or should we give back to people and to planet Earth? Should we pray for people? Should we make sacrifices for people? Should we help and love people? Should we like people? Should we hate people?

I did not want to go there, if there is a *there*. The possibility that there is a hell and that I may go to hell scared the hell out of me. I needed to lighten up my soul, clean it up, remove the dark shades, and get some pure white into my soul. I wanted to clean up my act and start being the best human being I could be so that I could convince the judge of my life that I am worthy of heaven and not worthy of hell.

All humans will be judged; therefore, all humans have an equal right to go to a good place or a bad place. Therefore, I must treat all humans equally, and I must love all humans as much as I love myself. Of course, if I do not love myself, I will have to fix that first. Then I will start not hating any human and eventually liking every human and ultimately loving every human. But I will begin with *"I WILL NOT HATE YOU."*

The soul is the scorecard or report card of how a human morally has behaved on planet Earth. The life test scorecard will not be judged on human terms but on God's terms. However, human self-judgment is the only means of testing you have for now.

After I die, I will have to face Jesus and look into His eyes. I will see the nail holes in His hands and feet and the spear gash in His side. I will see the thorn scars around His head and the places where flesh is missing from the scourging torture He endured. I will have to look in His loving eyes and convince Him that I am worthy of heaven or at least purgatory, but do not send me to hell. I will have to look in His eyes and convince Him that I loved him so much and I loved all humans so much that I am worthy to enter heaven.

Did I love and help others enough to deserve heaven? Was I meek and poor in spirit? Did I mourn? Was I hungry and thirsty? Was I merciful and clean of heart? Was I a peacemaker?

Did I suffer persecution for the sake of justice? Did I share my skills, generosity, time and extra bounty with other human beings? If there is a God, I do not want to go to hell. What can I do? I can start by not hating you. *"I will not hate you."*

CHAPTER THREE

How Did We Get Here?

But what if there is no God? Out of nothing something was created and developed this wonderful planet Earth full of energy, life and nature. When you are aviating a jet airplane at 35,000 feet above planet Earth, you acquire a different perspective: planet Earth looks smaller when you're looking down at it from seven miles above it. I have traveled to over 50 international cities and most of the cities in the United States of America.

I have flown around the world eastbound and around the world westbound. I have flown from Tokyo to Anchorage, and while flying through thirteen time zones I have seen Mother Nature's beautiful sunrise and sunset during the same flight. I have seen the Aurora Borealis, shooting stars, meteor showers, comets, beautiful and ferocious thunderstorms, volcanoes, every cloud type, every precipitation type, and all forms of terrain: sea, land, mountains, valleys, deserts, lakes, cities, farms and several wonders of the world.

I have flown from Anchorage over the North Pole to London and have observed the optical illusion of the Sun moving around planet Earth and depicting noon at various points on the planet. Through my extensive travels, numerous times I have been wowed by this wonderful planet

Earth, so full of energy and nature. I have wondered about the origins of our planet.

Out of nothing, something was created and developed beautiful sophisticated human beings that have a conscience and morality and can reason. Over my thirty-six years of flying, I have flown with over 1000 diverse pilots and met thousands of other distinctive people throughout my travels. Topography and manmade structures change throughout this planet Earth, but people are generally the same worldwide.

Physically, humans may look very different from outside appearances, but the DNA makeup of all humans is 99.9 percent identical. We beautiful, sophisticated humans are wonderfully made. I have pondered over the origins of our human race.

Amongst all Earth's species humans are able to communicate, create, build, advance, become more civilized and much more. The only conclusion is there must be some superhuman being, some creator and a god that initiated, created, and manipulated this process of evolution toward our existence today. "The most economical reliable explanation for why the universe is so precisely fine-tuned is because a creator – god – made it that way.

Can we credit just luck as a credible deduction for the origination of life?"[3] The Earth's size, distance from the sun, atmospheric conditions, its water, and even the position of our moon to us is perfectly aligned to allow our existence that only a creator, a god, could have enabled the perfectly arranged complexity of our planet and universe. The complexity of the human body, especially the brain and heart with DNA code programmed to instruct each cell in our body, points to a superhuman being, a god, that created the start of this process. Out of nothing, something emerged. The universe and our planet, with its uniform

15

laws of nature, had a start. What or who caused the start? A god did.

"If the law of gravity varied just slightly, the Universe would not be habitable for life. In relation to other forces in nature, gravity must be fine-tuned to one part in 10+40 (that's one part in 10,000000000000000000000000)."[4] As Cambridge physicist Stephen Hawking said, "if the rate of expansion one second after the Big Bang had been smaller by even one part in the hundred thousand million million, the universe would have re-collapsed before it reached its present size."[5]

There are actually nineteen such universal constants that must each be perfectly fine-tuned.[6] The odds against our being here are vanishingly small. According to Oxford physicist Roger Penrose, "If we jointly considered all the laws of nature that must be fine-tuned, we would be unable to write down such an enormous number, since the necessary digits would be greater than the number of the elementary particles in the universe."[7] The evidence for design is so compelling that Paul Davies, a renowned physicist at Arizona State University, has concluded that the bio-friendly nature of our universe looks like a "fix." "The cliché that life is balanced on the knife edge is a staggering understatement in this case: no knife in the universe could have an edge that fine."[8]

"No scientific explanation for the universe can be complete without accounting for this overwhelming appearance of design. Some try to explain away the fine-tuning by positing the existence of multiple universes, but the empirical evidence for such universes is nonexistent. The most economical reliable explanation for why the universe is so precisely fine-tuned is that our creator-god made it that way."[9] Some super-powerful being started, created and manipulated from nothing, leading to what we have on this planet Earth today—a god did.

Jesus revealed to us that there is a God. But was there a Jesus? Was Jesus just a crazy guy or was he a liar? Did Jesus die for a lie, and why?

Throughout Jesus's ministry, Jesus proclaimed that there is a God and that He was the Son of God. Jesus was killed for His teachings and beliefs. He had many chances, even just before He was condemned to death by Pontius Pilate, to claim He was a crazy guy or that His sayings were all lies so He could avoid a terrible death by crucifixion. The logical deduction is that Jesus was not insane, that He was telling the truth and that He died for this truth.

Did Jesus's apostles die for a lie, and if so, why? Jesus had twelve companions known as apostles who followed Jesus for three years prior to his death. Judas, one of the twelve apostles, hanged himself for betraying Jesus, and John, another apostle, died a natural death, but the remaining ten apostles were all killed for their beliefs and their preaching about Jesus Christ. Did they die for a lie or did they die for telling the truth about Jesus?

Saul of Tarsus (later to be called Paul the Apostle) was a Hebrew religious leader and a Roman citizen. Initially he persecuted the apostles, but then he experienced a vision from God and underwent a drastic conversion to follow and preach on behalf of Jesus. Paul's writings were included in the New Testament portion of the Bible. Paul was beheaded in Rome for his faith in Jesus. Did Paul die for a lie, or did he die for telling the truth about Jesus?

Writings about Jesus started to appear about 40 years after his death, in the letters of Paul and the Gospel of Mark. The Gospel of Matthew appeared about 55 years after Jesus's death, Luke's Gospel appeared after about 60 years, and John's Gospel appeared after about 65 years.

Matthew and John were two of the original twelve apostles. The Gospels of Matthew, Mark, Luke and John; written letters of Paul and others; the Acts of the Apostles; and the revelation of the Apocalypse describe Jesus's life, the way to salvation and the history of the new Christian religion. These writings, almost two thousand words, comprise the New Testament section of the Christian Holy Bible.[10] The Bible has remained the bestselling book of all time, providing supportive evidence that God and Jesus exist.

The earliest reference supporting the existence of Jesus, outside of pro-Christian writers, is found in *Antiquities of the Jews*, written by Josephus, a Roman Jewish scholar, around 65 years after the death of Jesus.[11] There is also the letter of Pliny the Younger to the Roman Emperor Trajan, writings from Tacitus, and writings from the Roman historian Suetonius around the same time.[12] Jesus is even mentioned in the Islamic Qur'an. Of course, for some people, a picture is more valuable proof and is worth a thousand words. For them there is the Shroud of Turin, the original burial cloth depicting a negative body image of the crucified Jesus.

So, if now you believe there is a God and you believe in Jesus, let's just assume Jesus had a mother, a mother called Mary. This book is not to prove to you there is a God and a Jesus. There is enormous written evidence proving that God exists and created Earth and us, and that Jesus exists. Jesus showed and taught us to love everyone, so this book is about you and me, calling us to not hate anyone. Therefore *"I will not hate you."*

CHAPTER FOUR

WHAT PEOPLE BELIEVE

Not all humans believe in Jesus and His teachings not to hate other people. What do other humans believe? Religion is a set of beliefs—usually in a superhuman being, a supernatural existence, or a god—generally agreed upon by a group of people. A religion usually includes a specific set of practices, rituals, observances, forms of worship, devotional services, prayers and/or a moral code of how to behave as a human being on this planet Earth. Most religions teach not to hate other humans. *I will not hate you.*

There are thousands of religions and sub-group religions, including new religions, extinct religions and even religions that formed from other religions: Christianity arose from Judaism and Buddhism arose from Hinduism, Babi and Baha'i arose from Islam and so forth.

Every religion is similar to some or all religions, and every religion is different from some or all religions. Currently the most widespread religions in the world in descending order are these:

> 1. There are over two billion Christians (including Roman Catholics, Protestants, Orthodox Christians and Anglicans).
>
> 2. There are almost two billion Muslims (including Shi'ite and Sunni).

3. Hindus account for over one billion followers.
4. Buddhists have fewer than half a billion followers.
5. Sikhs—around twenty million.
6. Judaism—around fifteen million.

There are agnostics that believe the existence of a god cannot be proven or disproven. Atheists believe that there is no god. There are approximately 200 million atheists worldwide—and a large population of approximately one billion who claim no religion at all.[13]

Just as there are various religions, there are several calendars that have been used throughout history. In the year 45 Before the Common Era (BCE), Julius Caesar added 67 days to the year and introduced 12 calendar months of 30 and 31 days, creating the Julian calendar. The Common Era (CE) or Anno Domini (AD) are based on "the year of our lord," or the year Jesus Christ was born, although historians believe Jesus may actually have been born four or six years earlier.

In the year 1582, Pope Gregory XIII reformed the Julian calendar, creating the Roman calendar (also known as the Gregorian calendar), because over time the Julian calendar had developed an error of about ten days. Today, most of the world uses the Gregorian calendar. While discussing the history of various religions, I have used several of these calendars to identify time in history.

Here is a short description and history of some of the major religions and prophets.

Hinduism is the major religion of India and is considered one of the oldest religions in the world, dating back to around 1500 BCE. Hinduism did not begin with a founder or a particular event, but over time evolved from various religious traditions that have existed throughout India's history. Hindus have many rituals, scriptures, and systems of beliefs, and they believe in millions of gods—yet each god is meant to help them reach Brahmin. Hindus believe that Brahmin is the principle and source of the universe. The Brahmin is a divine intelligence that penetrates all living beings, including the human soul and all living things that are embedded in the cosmic cycle of becoming (birth) and perishing (death).

They believe in the concept of reincarnation, in which, according to the Law of Karma, depending on how one conducts his or her moral behavior one can be reborn to a higher level of existence. Therefore, to conduct good behavior, it is best to not hate other people. *I will not hate you.* The Hindu society has a caste system that consists of five hereditary classes: Brahmin, Kshatriya, Vaishya, Shudra and the Untouchables. Some of the Hindu books date back to a thousand years BCE. Five of the main Hindu prayers or meditations are these:

1. Maha Mrityunjaya Mantra

2. Lord Shiva

3. Lord Ganesha

4. Sri Krishna

5. Sri Rama

Mahatma Gandhi was Hindu. The Ganges River is considered the most sacred place for Hindus.

Buddhism has its root in Hinduism. Siddhartha Gautama was a Hindu born into the Kshatriya caste in 560 BCE in what was then India and is now Nepal. After spending six wandering years living the most simplistic life, including daily fasting and meditation, at age 35 Siddhartha started a new religion known today as Buddhism.

Buddhists deny the existence of a human soul, but do not deny the existence of gods. The human person is at the center of Buddhism, and meditation is the method through which a person gains the two most important virtues: wisdom and compassion. To obtain the virtue of compassion one must start by not hating and then evolve to liking and ultimately to loving. *I will not hate you.*

Buddhists believe that through meditation one can realize that there is no permanence in life, and, ultimately, reach the spiritual goal of Nirvana. Reciting two of the most common forms of meditation, the "Mindfulness of Breath" and "Loving-Kindness" as well as saying the "Om Mani Padme Hum" mantra (a prayer), is a common practice. The Dalai Lama is a famous Buddhist monk. There are many famous Buddhist temples located in India, Indonesia, Thailand, Japan, Korea, Nepal and Myanmar.

Sikhism is a monotheistic religion (a one-god religion) that contains elements of both Hinduism and Islam. Sikhism was founded in the Punjab region by Guru Nanak in 1459 CE and had ten successive Sikh Gurus, of which Guru Granth Sahib provided the last holy scripture teaching. Sikhs believe in faith and justice in one god (Waheguru) and pursue salvation through disciplined personal meditation on the name and message of god. The Sikhs believe god can be realized through nature and through experiences and through other people; they believe that god has no beginning and no end and that god created all people equal. If we are all equal and I do not hate myself, then *I will not hate you.* Sikhism encourages sharing, giving and defending the rights of all creatures and all human beings.

Chinese Religions

For civil purposes, the Chinese use the Roman (Gregorian) Calendar, but for festivals the Chinese use their own Chinese calendar. The Chinese calendar was probably invented by Emperor Hungli in 2637 BCE, based on astronomical observations of the alignment of the sun and phases of the moon. Our Roman calendar year 2020 is the Chinese calendar year 4718, the year of the rat.

Chinese religions are a combination of Chinese folk religion, Taoism, Confucianism and Buddhism and have been closely related with the existing Chinese government.[14] The Shang Dynasty of 1500 BCE honored their ancestors, nature gods, weather gods and astrology, and believed the afterlife mirrored earthly life. This was the beginning of Chinese folk religion.

K'ung Fu-tzu (also known as Confucius) lived around 551 to 479 BCE, and through his teachings he tried to revitalize Chinese society based on his knowledge of ancient Chinese values and rituals. Confucius tried to instill morality and reduce the chaos that he perceived existed in China at the time. He wrote many of his teachings in a book called the Analects. The Han dynasty (from 206 BCE–220 CE) required the teachings of Confucius as mandatory in all schools.

Confucianism is a form of character formation in which one could obtain perfection as a "superior human." Confucianism believes in social order and that humans are naturally good. If you are naturally good then you are not bad, and *I will not hate you*. Confucianism emphasizes education and virtues.

The beginnings of **Taoism** probably started around 2000 BCE, but it was Lao-Tzu around 500 BCE who is credited as the founder of Taoism. Lao-Tzu wrote the "Tao-Te Ching" ("The Way and Its Power"). The Taoists believe that human achievements are foolish. They advise people to live simply, to live in harmony with nature, and to live in harmony with the Yin (the shaded dark bad) and the Yang (the sunny good). *I will not hate you*, and that will help me to live in harmony with you. Taoists believe in the "go with the flow" mentality, "the way" or "the nature of things." Taoists believe that actual physical immortality is a reachable goal. Many Chinese Taoist, Buddhist and Confucian temples were destroyed or taken over by the government during the Chinese communist revolution.

The **Japanese** were influenced by the Chinese religions. Buddhism flourished in Japan. These beliefs mixed with the Japanese **Shinto** beliefs. *Shinto was a name given to Japanese ethnic religion by the Chinese.*

The Shintoists believe in spirits called Kami, and this spiritual force of power exists in all things, especially nature, and is considered "the way of gods."[15] Shintoists believe in harmony, purity and loyalty. Shintoists believe that the world is overflowing with Kami—and that all life, all creation, and human nature are generally good. Human nature is generally good; therefore, *I will not hate you*.

The Kojiki and Nihon Shoki are two of the sacred Japanese writings of the eighth century BCE. The emperor was the sacred leader of Japan until the end of World War II. The Grand Shrine of Ise is the most sacred of places for the Shintoists.

Abrahamic Religions

According to the book of Genesis, God made a covenant with Abraham. Abraham was a great prophet from around 1800 BCE who is recognized by three major religions: Christianity, Islam and Judaism.[16] Abraham was a nomadic tribesman and a shepherd who traveled extensively from what today is called Iraq to what today is called Palestine.

Abraham begot Ishmael with his Egyptian slave servant Hagar (eventually sending them away) and Abraham begot Isaac with his wife Sarah. The three-thousand-year-old Jewish religion began with the prophet Abraham, as written in the Torah, which is part of the Hebrew Bible (the Tanakh)[17] or what Christians call the Old Testament. This Bible contains 39 books containing almost 6,000 words, and was inspired by great prophets, including Moses, David, Isaiah, Jeremiah, Ezekiel and many others.[18] Included in the Jewish Bible are 613 laws that Jews must follow, including the famous Ten Commandments that their greatest prophet, Moses, reportedly received directly from God.

The Ten Commandments—Exodus 20:2–17

> 1. You shall not have other gods beside me.
>
> 2. You shall not make for yourself an idol or a likeness of anything.
>
> 3. You shall not invoke the name LORD, your God in vain.
>
> 4. Remember the Sabbath day—keep it holy.
>
> 5. Honor your father and your mother.
>
> 6. You shall not kill.
>
> 7. You shall not commit adultery.
>
> 8. You shall not steal.
>
> 9. You shall not bear false witness against your neighbor.
>
> 10. You shall not covet your neighbor's house. You shall not covet your neighbor's wife, his male or

female slave, his ox or donkey, or anything that belongs to your neighbor.[19]

Commandments numbers 5 thru 10 maintain that you should not be bad to other people and you should not hate other people. *I will not hate you.*

The **Jews** believe in one God who is eternal, who knows all thoughts and deeds of men, and who will reward the good and punish the wicked. Accordingly, one should pray to the one God, follow the written Torah and the words of the prophets, especially the greatest prophet, Moses. The Jews believe that there is a Messiah who will come someday, and the dead will be resurrected. However, in Judaism, actions are more important than beliefs. Jerusalem is their most sacred place.[20]

Christianity started around 8–6 BCE with the birth of Jesus and the belief that Jesus was the Messiah, the Christ. As discussed earlier, the Christian Holy Bible includes two major sections, the Old Testament (the Jewish Hebrew Bible) and the New Testament (God made a new covenant with the people) that included 27 more books and almost 2,000 more words. The New Testament includes the four Gospels of Matthew, Mark, Luke and John, describing Jesus's life and the way to salvation; the history of the new Christian religion; written letters of Paul and others; and the revelation of the Apocalypse.[21]

Who was this Jesus guy? Why should we believe in Jesus? *Supposedly Jesus was born in an obscure village to a peasant woman and a stepfather over 2,000. He grew up in another obscure village, where He worked as a carpenter until He was about thirty years old.*[22] Then He left home, picked 12 companions, and became a traveling preacher for about three years.

Supposedly He performed many miracles. He was a peaceful man and taught people to love God and everyone.

If you cannot love everyone, try to like everyone, but do not hate anyone. *I will not hate you.* Jesus taught the people the "Our Father" prayer and two new commandments:

The Golden rule—Matthew 7:12 "Do to others whatever you would have them do to you."

The Great Commandment—Luke 10:27 "You shall love the Lord your God with all your heart, with all your being, with all your strength, and with all your mind; and your neighbor as yourself."

Jesus never had a family or owned a home. He never set foot inside a big city. He never traveled more than 200 miles from the place he was born. He never wrote a book or held an office or did any of the usual things that accompany greatness.[23]

While He was still a young man, approximately 33 years old, His popularity changed. His friends deserted Him and denied Him. *He was turned over to his enemies. He went through a mockery of a trial, was tortured, made to carry His own cross and nailed to that cross between two thieves.*[24]

While He was dying on the cross, His executioners gambled for the only piece of property He had—His coat. After He died, He was taken down and laid in a borrowed grave. Supposedly three days later He rose from the dead, taught his apostles for an additional forty days, and then ascended to heaven.

His apostle Peter, along with the other apostles, spread the Christian religion and is now claimed as the first pope by the Roman Catholic Church (RCC). *Twenty centuries have come and gone*, and today Jesus is the central figure for much of the human race; approximately two billion people believe in Him. *All the armies that ever marched and all the navies that ever sailed and all the parliaments that ever sat, and all the kings that ever reigned,* put together, have not affected the life of man upon this earth as powerfully as this one solitary life of Jesus.²⁵

I like Jesus. I admire Jesus. I love Jesus Christ!

Christians believe *there is a God who sent his son, Jesus, to save the world*—John 3:17. Today there are various Christian denominations and beliefs, but many churches, including the Roman Catholic Christians (RCCs), believe in *God the Father almighty, Creator of heaven and earth. And in Jesus Christ, God's only Son, their Lord, Who was conceived by the Holy Spirit, born of the Virgin Mary, suffered under Pontius Pilate, was crucified, died, and was buried. Jesus descended into hell; the third day He rose again from the dead. He ascended into heaven, and sits at the right hand of God the Father almighty; from thence He shall come to judge the living and the dead.*

He will judge you and me. If the vision of hell is real, then I do not want to go to hell. One way of avoiding hell is to start by not hating others. *I will not hate you.*

The prayer continues: *I believe in the Holy Spirit, the holy Catholic Church, the communion of saints, the forgiveness of sins, the resurrection of the body and life everlasting.*²⁶ The Pope is the RCCs' religious leader, and he resides in the Vatican in Rome, Italy. The popes' succession can be traced back to the first pope, Peter the Apostle.

The Holy Bible (Old and New Testaments) is a collection of books (and songs) written by many authors inspired by God and describing God's interactions with people and nations. The Bible can be considered part fictional and non-fictional, and includes poetry, narration and prophecy. Therefore, when reading the Holy Bible, we need to interpret some texts literally, some texts symbolically and some texts historically. The Bible has been translated into over 100,000 languages and is always one of the top ten best-selling books.

Like Judaism and Christianity, **Islam** is a monotheistic religion. It holds that Muslims are heirs of Abraham. Remember Hagar (the handmaid servant of Abraham's wife Sarah) and Hagar's son, Ishmael, who were sent away? Muslims believe that Ishmael and his lineage settled in Mecca, Saudi Arabia.

The Arab prophet Muhammad was born around 560 CE in Mecca. Muhammad considered himself the last of the prophets of Islam—the last in a line of seven prophets, with Abraham as the first prophet, and Jesus as prophet number six. Muhammad preached complete submission to one true God, a God he called Allah. He cleansed the ancient Ka'aba shrine of idol worship and rebuilt and rededicated it to Allah.

He believed the angel Gabriel gave him many revelations, which he memorized and had other people memorize. These recitations became the oral text of the Qur'an throughout Muhammad's lifetime. Eventually, after Mohammad's death, the oral memorized text of the Qur'an was recorded by Abu Bakr (around 634 CE) and Utham (around 650 CE).

Muslims believe every idea or action must be centered on the oneness of God and that the Qur'an is the direct word of God. Muslims must express their belief through the duties of the Five Pillars of Islam: profession of faith, prayer, fasting, almsgiving and pilgrimage. Muslims believe attention to God and caring for others are very important duties. Almsgiving and caring for other people suggest not hating other people. *I will not hate you.*

At age 26, I was operating a B 747 Jumbo Jet on a ten-day trip around the world. The itinerary was New York to Brussels (The Netherlands) to Dubai (near Saudi Arabia) to Hong Kong to Tokyo to Anchorage to Chicago and back to

New York. The flight crew had a two-day layover in Dubai. Dubai is a Middle Eastern city in the United Arab Emirates, located on the Persian Gulf adjacent to the Arabian Desert. Dubai is about 1,100 miles from Mecca, the birthplace of the Muslim religion and Muslims' most important sacred place.

During my layover in Dubai, I toured the fish market and the Gold Souk; using their currency, called the Dirham, I purchased and tasted fantastically cooked kabobs with pita bread. My eyes fixed on the women in Dubai who wore long black robes with headscarves that cover their neck and part of their head. Most of the women had their faces covered, exposing only their eyes. In this part of the world, religion has laws outlining ways in which women live their lives on a day-to-day basis. I heard the "call to prayer" horn alerting people to one of the designated five times a day one must turn toward Mecca and pray to Allah.

I felt compassion for a man whose left hand had been cut off, and after an inquiry I learned he had been found guilty of stealing with that hand, and his punishment was having his hand cut off. The locals explained to me that they still occasionally have hangings on the third Thursday of the month. The legal system is based on the government's official interpretation of Islamic law, and all citizens are required to be Muslims.

Is this what it was like during Jesus's time? As I ventured throughout the city the ambience of the culture, people and structures inspired my imagination of a time and place during which Jesus was living. As I meandered into one beautiful, ancient building, I envisioned a young Jesus sitting in the temple courts amongst the teachers, listening and asking questions.

I did not know that I was in a holy mosque, a place where Muslims worship, study and discuss Islam. Within minutes I was chased out; to enter you must remove your footwear and wear appropriate clothing. This was my first experience of being exposed to a religion that was extremely different from my Christian religion. But still, like me, they believed *"I will not hate you."*

Other Faiths

The Baha'i Faith, one of the newest religions, was founded by Bahá'u'lláh in the 1880s in Persia. Baha'i seems to have emerged from a combination of early religious beliefs, mainly Islam. Messengers such as Abraham, the Buddha, Jesus, Muhammad and others have been included. This is a monotheistic religion that emphasizes the spiritual unity of God, the unity of religion and the unity of all mankind.

How can mankind unite if we hate each other? *I will not hate you.* Followers of Baha'i believe that God periodically reveals His will through divine messengers in order to transform the character of humankind and to develop their moral and spiritual qualities.

The Mormon faith (or the Church of Jesus Christ of Latter-Day Saints) is another relatively new religion started by Joseph Smith Jr. in the 1820s in the United States. Mormonism is a Christian faith that recognizes more of the recent prophets rather than all of the prophets that most other Christians recognize. The Book of Mormon, together with its interpretation of the Bible, are the two primary sources of the Mormon faith. Mormons believe that Native Americans are one of the lost tribes of Israel, and they believe that someday Jesus will return to Earth and set up a New Jerusalem in America and will reign for 1,000 years. Mormons believe in Jesus, and Jesus taught us to love one another. *I will not hate you.*

There are many lesser-known religions, such as African Yoruba, Santeria, Candomblés, Shango, Voodoo and Australian Aboriginal, to name just a few. There are agnostics who are undecided on whether God exists, and atheists who believe that a god does not exist at all. Most if not all religions teach their followers to love people and not hate people. *"I will not hate you."*

CHAPTER FIVE

PRAY TO NOT HATE

Most religions preach about what may happen after death. Who really knows what happens when you die? Hedge your bets—God may really exist and is about to judge your soul. You may die today or you may die tomorrow, but you will die and you will be judged. I think the soul is a scorecard of how we morally lived on planet Earth.

There are seven billion human beings and over a billion species from the simplest of living organisms to large mammals on our planet Earth. Earth is just one of the nine planets in our solar system. We are just one solar system in the Milky Way galaxy of stars. There are billions of other galaxies in our universe. There must be some superhuman higher intellectual being who exists—let's call him God (call him Lord or Allah, if you prefer)—but there is only one God.

Now read the Holy Bible, the Torah, the Qur'an, the Analects of Confucius, the Tao Te-Ching, the Tripitaka, the Bhagovad-Gita, the Book of Mormon, et cetera. Now, come on. Some spirit must have influenced those writers to write insights into some type of god. So, there must be a god.

What is the downside in believing and praying to a god? What is the downside in trying every day to not hate any person at any time? If there is a god, and he or she provides us life twenty-four hours a day, seven days a week, then I will hedge my bets and pray at least an hour a day and honor him or her at least an hour a week.

There are over 200 Christian denominations. I chose to be a Christian believer only because of what this Jesus guy said. You can throw out the whole Bible and throw all of the religions out the window, but I will accept and believe and attempt to do the two things Jesus said: love God and love all human beings the same. And I will add one more thing: love yourself. If you do not love yourself, how can you love God and/or anyone? How can you begin to not hate?

So here are the three things I tell myself:

1. Love God.

2. Love yourself (if you do not love yourself, change so that you will love yourself).

3. Love all people (no matter what, try to love everyone). If you love God, self and others, then you will comply with the Ten Commandments, the Qur'an and the other major religious doctrines. There will also be peace among all people on planet Earth. Start today and repeat after me, "*I will not hate you.*" "*I will not hate you.*" "*I will not hate you.*"

Jesus and the other prophets taught us to pray. It is important to pray prayers for help and gratitude. We should pray prayers to help us not hate the other person, to help us like the other person and maybe love the other person. Here are some prayers and my prayer. That Jesus guy gave us a prayer (the Lord's Prayer, also called the Our Father prayer).

Here are two versions of the Our Father prayer.

Our father, Who art in heaven,

Hollow be thy Name.
Thy kingdom come.
Thy will be done on earth, as it is in heaven.
Give us this day our daily bread,
and forgive us our trespasses,
as we forgive those who trespass against us,
and lead us not into temptation,
but deliver us from evil. Amen.[27]
(This version is based on passages from Luke 11:2–4 and Matthew 6:9–13.)

Our father in heaven,
Reveal who you are.
Set the world right,
Do what's best—
As above, so below.
Keep us alive with three square meals.
Keep us forgiven with you and forgiving others.
Keep us safe from ourselves and the devil.
You're in charge!
You can do anything you want!
You're ablaze in beauty!
Yes. Yes. Yes.[28]
(This is a version from *The Message//Remix* by Eugene H. Peterson).

Notice: God forgive me and I will forgive others. *I will not hate you.*

This prayer by Saint Francis of Assisi is a prayer that followers of most religions of the world would probably feel comfortable saying:

Lord, make me an instrument of your peace;
Where there is hatred, let me sow love;

Where there is injury, pardon,
Where there is doubt, faith;
Where there is despair, hope:
Where there is darkness, light;
And where there is sadness, joy.
Grant that I may not so much seek
To be consoled as to console;
To be understood as to understand;
To be loved as to love;
For it is in giving that we receive;
It is in pardoning that we are pardoned;
And it is in dying that we are born to eternal life.[29]

Saint Francis (I like his name), a Christian, was born in Assisi, Italy, in 1182. He loved pleasure, wore expensive clothes and spent money lavishly until he received an inspirational dream from God. He then changed his life drastically by living very modestly and giving to and helping the poor. Among other accomplishments, Saint Francis started the Franciscan Friars and the Christmas Nativity tradition. He loved God, all people, all animals and all living creatures. Francis did not hate anyone or anything. *I will not hate you.*

Lao-Tzu, the founder of Taoism, wrote this:

If there is to be peace in the world,
There must be peace in the nations.
If there is to be peace in the nations,
There must be peace in the cities.
If there is to be peace in the cities,
There must be peace between neighbors.
If there is to be peace between neighbors,
There must be peace in the home.
If there is to be peace in the home,

There must be peace in the heart.[30]

I will not hate you. Praying helps me to not hate you. Here is a prayer that I wrote, and I say or attempt to say it daily. Actually, I say it nightly before my body succumbs to sleep. I change and customize the blank lines as necessary.

One of the original reasons I wrote the "Trinity for Me" prayer was that in the summer of 2009 I did not have time to pray the other traditional prayers because I was studying. Pilots are always studying to prepare for a flight, prepare for possible emergencies, prepare for a simulator check ride, to learn changing jet aircraft systems technology or to learn a new jet airplane. Every six months pilots are required by federal law to take a simulator check ride consisting of multiple complicated emergency tasks that you rarely and hopefully never encounter, but if you should encounter such an emergency, you would be prepared and be able to survive. One example of such an emergency was Sully Sullenberger's miracle on the Hudson. If you fail this flight check ride, you could be out of a job, so there is great pressure to perform to the flight standards as required by federal law.

If an airline pilot upgrades to a captain position or upgrades to another jet airplane, that pilot will have to go to flight school and train for several months. The pilot must pass a written test, an oral test, several simulator flight tests and several in-flight tests. If you should fail any of these tests, it is possible to lose your job or be demoted. Pilots are the most regulated professionals in the USA, and airline flight standards are very high.

In 2009, while I was in flight training for an Airbus widebody jet airplane captain's position, I only had time to sleep, eat, rarely exercise, and study, study, study and study. I did not have time to pray the traditional prayers, so I wrote the

"Trinity For Me" prayer. In a nutshell, "thank you for and help me with."

TRINITY FOR ME

> *O my dear God*
> *O my dear Jesus*
> *And the Holy Spirit,*
> *Thank You for this moment of life.*
> *Thank You for this breath of air.*
> *Thank You for providing water and food for my body,*
> *And thank You for protecting, guiding, and nourishing my soul.*
> *Thank You for _____.*
> *Please help and/or grant me this request_____.*
> *Please protect and guide my thoughts, words, heart, and soul*
> *Toward you during this earthly journey so that after this life I will be in heaven.*
> *Please help me to love God, myself, and everyone.*
> *I love you, trust you, believe in you, and hope to be with you.*
> *Amen.*

Jesus taught us the way to pray with the Lord's Prayer, also known as the Our Father. The Lord's Prayer is the gold standard of all prayers given to us from the Son of God, and this is the most important prayer to pray first. The *"Trinity for Me"* is my special prayer, and I hope that this prayer will become your special prayer. The appendix includes a copy of this prayer for you to use. You can use this prayer and customize the contents of the blank lines or write your own prayer.

A prayer is a deeply sincere request or devout petition for help or an expression of thanks to a God or an object of worship. Most prayers include praise, a petition, an intercession and thanksgiving. God, thank you for whatever, if You will it, help me with whatever, and I will try to love you, myself and everyone else. But most of all, help me to not hate anyone. *I will not hate you.*

CHAPTER SIX

"TRINITY FOR ME" DISSECTED

I believe I was spiritually influenced when I wrote the "Trinity for Me" prayer. I believe the Holy Spirit inspired me to learn these words and apply these words to my heart and to the hearts of others. The following was my thought process on where the words came from, what the words mean, and how you can use this prayer. To be sure, the "Lord's Prayer" is the first go-to prayer given to us by Jesus.

At the end of my day before my human body falls asleep, I reflect on my day and say prayers. Usually the transition from waking to sleeping takes about five to fifteen minutes for my body to settle down. This is an opportune time for reflection and to pray prayers.

When I am dead tired and short on time sometimes, I just pray the "Trinity for Me" prayer to sum up my life that day. What am I thankful for and how can God help me, if He wills it? Who did I not love today and how can God help me better to love, better to like and not to hate that person or persons? God help me to not hate anyone. *I will not hate you.*

TRINITY FOR ME

O my dear God

God is first, God is number one. There are seven billion human beings and over a billion species from the simplest of living organisms to large mammals on our planet Earth. Earth is just one of the eight planets with the sun in our solar system. We are just one solar system in the Milky Way galaxy of stars. There are billions of other galaxies in our universe. There must be some superhuman higher intellectual being who exists—let's call him God (call him Lord or Allah, if you prefer)—but there is only one God.

God is number one. God is the reason we are here. Out of nothing, something was created and developed into the sophisticated human being. There must be a God. Will you agree with me that there is a creator?

O my dear Jesus

Jesus taught us how to love. So, we can prove historically that there was a Jesus and He was crucified. There is tremendous evidence that He rose from the dead and started one of the most widespread religions, with over two billion followers. There are numerous stories of great miracles He performed, such as healing and curing the sick, the crippled and the possessed. But most importantly, *oh my dear Jesus* showed and taught us how to love.

He was born under the poorest conditions and did not accumulate any wealth or material goods. He became very popular and then was deserted by His friends and killed. Yes, He forgave His friends; He forgave His persecutors and He loved everyone.

He loved His mother, He loved His group of followers, He loved children, He loved the old and the sick and He loved His enemies. He loved all humans so much that He died for our sins so that we may have a chance to get to heaven. *Oh, my dear Jesus*, thank you for loving us and showing us how to love.

And the Holy Spirit,

The Holy Spirit, or some say the Holy Ghost, has influenced many of great prophets to write on God's behalf. God through the Holy Spirit influenced all the authors of the Bible. I believe the Holy Spirit inspired me to write this prayer and this book. The Holy Spirit is the force that connects us. The Holy Spirit connects us to Jesus and Jesus to God, and God to us, and God to Jesus. Consider the Holy Spirit as the force of Earth's life energy that connects us to the spiritual world.

Thank You for this moment of life.

Most of us know what day we were born. Your parents probably told you what day you were born, and you may even have an official birth certificate indicating where and when you were born. Most of us don't know what day we will die.

Twice within the year 1995, I was involved in saving someone's life. Once while in Cabo Roig, Spain, I helped a Spanish man survive a heart attack. Six months later in our home, I helped my wife survive a ruptured brain aneurysm.

Be grateful for this moment of life, because life is precious, valuable, delicate and unpredictable. Be grateful for this moment of life, because you do not know when your last moment of life will be.

Thank You for this breath of air.

Breathe, breathe in the air. We breathe air, and air directly or indirectly supports every form of life on planet Earth. The body must always be able to take in good air and get rid of bad air. When the body cannot do this, the body will suffocate and we will die.

Thank You for providing water and food for my body,

Pure water is transparent, odorless and tasteless, and consists of hydrogen and oxygen (H_2O). Water is the most critical and most important nutrient. Death occurs when a person loses 20 percent of total body water. Most people would be able to live only about a week without water.

The human body may require up to about six to eight glasses of water per day. The body consists largely of water; between 50 and 75 percent of a person's body weight is made up of water. Water helps hydrate the body and flushes out impurities. Pure water contains no calories, whereas all other fluids contain at least some calories.

Food is one of our most basic needs. Food supplies the nutrients that the human body needs for providing energy, building and repairing tissues, and regulating body processes. Water, carbohydrates, fats, proteins, minerals and vitamins are the essential nutrients your body needs to survive. No single food supplies every necessary nutrient. However, the sweet potato may contain more beneficial nutrients than any other single food item.

Food comes mainly from plants (grains, fruit, vegetables, et cetera) or from animals that eat plants (meats, eggs, milk, et cetera). Most people could live only 60 to 70 days without food. How long a person can survive without food depends on the person's supply of body fat.

And thank You for protecting, guiding and nourishing my soul.

What do we know about the body and soul? After all these years of doctors performing surgeries and dissections on the human body, no one has found the human soul. The soul is that spiritual and moral thought, action, emotion and will. The soul may be our scorecard of how we morally live on planet Earth. After death, we may have to submit our scorecard to a judge to decide if we are worthy of heaven or hell. I believe everyone has a soul.

"What good will it be for someone to gain the whole world, yet forfeit their *soul*? Or what can anyone give in exchange for their *soul*?" (Matthew 16:26).

"Do not be afraid of those who kill the body but cannot kill the *soul*; rather, be afraid of the one who can destroy both soul and body in Gehenna." Gehenna is a place that symbolized hell (Matthew 10:28).

"Beloved, I hope you are prospering in every respect and are in good health, just as your *soul* is prospering" (3 John 2).

"Love the Lord, your God, with all your heart, with all your *soul*, and with all your mind" (Matthew 22:37).

Thank You for _____.(Customize to your situation)

Giving Thanks

Customize and fill in the blank according to your situation. It's always a good idea to take stock of the good things—and to express thanks. I am so lucky I have more than most people even though I may not have as much as some.

I have my life today. I can breathe, drink, eat and sleep. I have my religion. I have my health. I have my family and friends. I have a home and I am able to provide for my family. A roof over my head and food on the table and everything or anything else is extra.

Thank you for keeping my sons and wife safe and healthy. Thank you for my health. Thank you for my wife, sons, family and friends. Thank you for my ability to provide for my family.

Thank you for my ability to help people through philanthropy. Thank you for my intelligence and imagination, sense of humor, compassion, sympathy and love. Thank you for all the various people and Mother Nature on this planet Earth. Thank you for my garden and the food I am able to grow, harvest, consume and share with others. Thank you for my boat and the ability and opportunity to catch fish to eat (Jesus was a fisherman, too).

Thank you for the use of my brain to imagine and dream about life. As an escape, I am able to imagine people, places, and things, great occasions and fun times. Thank you for my heart and compassion. I can pray for you, myself and anyone or everyone. I can love, give love and be loved. Giving and getting love feels great.

Thank you for helping me to not hate you or anyone else. Thank you for answering my previous prayer requests.

Please help and/or grant me this request_____. (Customize to your situation)

Customize and fill in the blank according to your situation. Everyone needs help sometimes. Maybe you have a White Knight who will be there all the time to help you. Maybe one day that White Knight cannot help you with your particular problem.

Maybe there is no human who can help you. Maybe you need superhuman help. Maybe there is a God, a Creator who can help you. So, I want to add my name to a Help Pie with this prayer.

Help Pie-Request

Dear God, I know you have many requests for help: Help in healing the sick, removing or reducing pain and suffering, eradicating viruses, stopping war and crime. Help to deal with loss of loved ones, healing mental illness, forgiving sins and letting souls into heaven. Help to improve marriage and family relationships, and many greater requests for help.

I know you have a great many requests for help from others throughout the world, but please grant me my help-worth or portion of my help request. I know the "Help Pie-Request" is large, but please grant me a small portion of help from the "Help Pie-Request" list. Whenever someone asks me how I'm doing, I reply:

> "Better than most but not as good as some."
> "What do you mean?" they might ask.
> When someone asks me, I will say:
> Whatso has no job so
> Everwhat has no hut.
> Notwhy is hungry and dry.
> Realget is unhealthy and upset.
> Realget lost his breath and is facing death.
> Say-don't-you lost his I love you.
> Guysyou is all-alone with no you.
> Guys you is all-alone with no "I have you" or "I love you."
> Ycraz darkened his soul and entered a no-religion phase.
> Youhey cannot endure the pain anymore or any way.
> Comehow hurt me really bad somehow.
> That's why.

In life there is always someone in worse shape than you, and there is always someone doing better than you. On this planet Earth, everyone lives in his or her own world, and sometimes that world can feel like a prison, in a way. Each person's prison is defined differently.

You may be in a marriage or a relationship, and the other partner is constantly arguing and complaining and is never pleased. Maybe he or she always wants more money to spend. You may have a disability. You may have physical health issues or mental health issues. You may be poor, hungry, weeping, hated, lonely, insulted or all of the above.

My suggestion? Focus on the good things around you, on what is going well. Don't worry so much and try to be happy. When you are not worrying and you are happy, you are more able to not hate others.

Jesus said: "Therefore I tell you, do not worry about your life, what you will eat [or drink], or about your body, what you will wear. Is not life more than food, and the body more than clothing? Look at the birds in the sky; they do not sow or reap, they gather nothing into barns, yet your heavenly Father feeds them. Are not you more important than they? Can any of you by worrying add a single moment to your life-span?" (Matthew 6:25–27).

There are no mistakes in life; everything is meant to happen for a reason. It's okay to make a mistake. Learn from that mistake and don't make the same mistake twice. If all hell breaks loose, don't worry, be happy; remember, you can always laugh and sing. In fact, here's a song I wrote:

Sing a Song

>Tell me a lot about singing a song;
>Singing a song helps getting along.
>Doesn't matter what kind of song,
>Rhyming or not, short or long, right or wrong.
>As long as you're singing your song
>Life seems better, and less and less seems wrong.
>When you are feeling unhappy and down

Start moving your mouth around and sing your song.
Now that you know you need your own song,
Time to produce and write your best personal song.

I or someone else I know may have physical health issues, mental health issues or relationship issues. I or someone else I know may be poor, hungry, weeping, hated, lonely, insulted or all of the above. God, if you will it, please help them with ___. Please help me to not hate you, anyone or myself.

Please protect and guide my thoughts, words, heart and soul toward you during this earthly journey so that after this life I will be in heaven.

I am only human, and I need help with my thoughts, words, heart and soul day in and day out. I am not strong enough, and my faith is not as strong as Jesus's faith. Help me to think good thoughts, to say kind words, to love and to maintain a clean soul. I need help to get to heaven. I do not want to go to that dreadful hell that was described in the beginning of this book. I need help to not hate anyone.

Please help me to love God, everyone, and myself.

Jesus summarized his view on love for God, everyone and myself with this double commandment: "You shall love the Lord, your God, with all your heart, with all your soul, and with all your mind" and "You shall love your neighbor as yourself" (Matthew 22:37–39, Mark 12:30–31 and Luke 10:27).

Of course, you must look in the mirror and decide if you like what you see. How can you love others as yourself if you do not love yourself? Make the changes in your life so that when you look in the mirror you will love yourself. Then you can love others as yourself.

I love you, trust you, believe in you and hope to be with you.

"So now faith, hope, love remain, these three; but the greatest of these is love" (1 Corinthians 13:13). I love You. I believe You exist and trust You will help me. I hope I am worthy to join You in heaven.

Amen.

The spoken word used to express solemn ratification, certainty, truth or agreement. "It is so," or "so let it be."

"I will not hate you."

CHAPTER SEVEN

JESUS TAUGHT US

Jesus showed and taught us how to not hate anyone. Jesus has shown us how to deal with hate. Jesus was born with nothing, he had nothing, all his friends left him and then he was brutally killed.

He showed us how to forgive, forget, love, and be peaceful. Jesus forgave Peter after Peter denied Him three times. Jesus forgave Peter and made him the leader of a new Christian religion. Jesus was mocked, tortured and falsely murdered, and He forgave those responsible.

We should be generous with our special gifts to help and not hate people. Jesus taught us to home the homeless, feed the hungry, be peaceful, forgive, love God and love everyone. Do not hate anyone. *I will not hate you.*

Jesus orated on a mountain, probably Mount Eremos, a list of guidelines to not hate humans. The guidelines are called the Beatitudes, or the blessings, deriving from the Latin word *beatus*. These Beatitudes described what certain groups of people were experiencing in their present lives and what they will experience in the future when they will be judged at the end of their life. Luke's version of the Beatitudes tends to emphasize physical hardship, while Matthew's version tends to emphasize internal struggles. Matthew's version is more popular; the text is as follows:

- Blessed are the poor in spirit, for theirs is the kingdom of heaven.
- Blessed are they who mourn, for they shall be comforted.
- Blessed are the meek, for they will inherit the land.
- Blessed are they who hunger and thirst for righteousness, for they will be satisfied.
- Blessed are the merciful, for they will be shown mercy.
- Blessed are the clean of heart, for they will see God.
- Blessed are the peacemakers, for they will be called children of God.
- Blessed are they who are persecuted for the sake of righteousness, for theirs is the kingdom of heaven.

(Matthew 5:3–10)

Was I poor in spirit, was I meek, did I mourn, did I hunger and thirst for righteousness, was I merciful, did I have a clean heart, was I a peacemaker, and did I suffer persecution for the sake of justice? In a nutshell, Jesus was saying that on judgment day, those who were personally well off will be condemned, and those who have suffered will be blessed. Those who do not heed Jesus's words may go to hell, as described in the beginning of this book.

The Beatitudes are guidelines for those who have, to help those who do not have, in order to improve their chances of avoiding hell. Using the different talents and things that God gave you, be generous with other people in need. *"I will not hate you."*

***

Here are some of Jesus's other famous lines on dealing with to not hate.

"Do not worry about tomorrow; tomorrow will take care of itself" (Matthew 6:34). Stress has physical and emotional effects on us, and some stress can create negative feelings. De-stress to help yourself to not hate. I will manage my stress and *"I will not hate you."*

"When someone slaps you on [your] right cheek, turn the other one to him as well" (Matthew 5:39). *"I will not hate you."*

"Let the one among you who is without sin be the first to throw a stone at her" (John 8:7). *"I will not hate you."*

"But I say to you, love your enemies, and pray for those who persecute you" (Matthew 5:44). *"I will not hate you."*

"You shall love the Lord, your God, with all your heart, with all your soul, and with all your mind. You shall love your neighbor as yourself. The whole law and the prophets depend on these two commandments" (Matthew 22:37–40). *"I will not hate you."*

"Do to others as you would have them do to you" (Luke 6:3). *"I will not hate you."*

CHAPTER EIGHT

WHY WE HATE

To hate someone is to dislike that person with extreme intensity. You may be intensely hostile to that person and detest everything about that person. My goal is to persuade you to not hate any humans, to like all humans or maybe to love all people.

To like someone is to display strong feelings of admiration and fondness toward that person. You may be kindly attracted to that person and enjoy everything about them. On the other hand, to love someone is to have the strongest feelings of affection for that person. You may be deeply, emotionally attracted to that person and persistently pursue a bonded relationship with them.

The Holy Bible says: "Love is patient, love is kind. It is not jealous, [love] is not pompous, it is not inflated, it is not rude, it does not seek its own interest, it is not quick-tempered, it does not brood over injury, it does not rejoice over wrongdoing but rejoices with truth. It bears all things, believes all things, endures all things. Love never fails" (1 Corinthians 13:4–8). *"I will not hate you."*

There are different ranges of hate, liking and love. Love for a friend, say in a romantic relationship, differs from love of a sibling, which differs from love for a spouse, which differs from love of a child. There's guest love, friendly love, platonic love, romantic love, family love, parental love, divine love and others.

Just as there are various ranges of love, love for a person can transform over time. When I first met Carmel, the woman who eventually became my wife, I was totally infatuated with her. Those infatuated feelings developed into romantic love, leading into the ultimate level of intimacy of making love to each other.

Then I experienced her motherly love when I fixated on my wife's eyes as she exuberantly gazed at our newborn son for the first time. Then we experienced parental love through all the good times and bad times of raising children. There are times your children can bring you the greatest joys and the most hurtful pains. The parental love for your children during those times when they are sick or injured can produce the most intense feelings of worry.

Then there was that time when my wife almost died. I prayed for her every hour and visited her daily while she was hospitalized in the intensive care unit. During this time, I realized how much I loved my spouse, and she was too young to leave me.

Presently my spouse and I are at that stage of love where we are helping each other survive the later stages of life. While visiting Alicante, Spain, we observed 90-year-old couples holding hands and walking the promenade. This form of love was the most motivating example to us of helping and supporting each other through various stages of age.

The range of human kindness can be measured by the level of unselfish, loyal concern for the good of a person. These are several reasons to love or like, but why do we hate?

"In time we hate that which we often fear."

William Shakespeare

One reason we hate is that we fear people who are different from us, especially when we do not know anything about them. People hate what they don't understand. People reject those who think differently and look different from us.

When we get the impression that the other person doesn't seem to fit into our social circle, we may feel threatened by the outsider and will not welcome them and will dislike them. If a new person joins your group, others within that group may feel threatened that that individual will change the group, and they may show a shared hatred toward the new person. We have a strong love for our social group and an aggression for the other group because that group is different, may be dangerous, and may be a threat to our group.

Some people hate out of a desire for friendship and belonging. They may join a hate group to fulfill a need of friendship and belonging by putting down others outside of their group. The hate group unites people to act against what they perceive to be a common enemy, whether real or imagined.

The members within the group may increase their sense of well-being and self-esteem as they jointly hate others. In such cases, becoming enraged and hating a person or persons is motivated by other members of the group. Mutual dislike produces a stronger response than mutual like. Group members may become cruel, judgmental and antisocial, and they may make negative statements about other people they perceive as different from them.

"From the deepest desires often comes the deadliest hate."

Socrates

We are wired to see people outside our group as enemies. Our brains' negative bias toward outsiders evolved because it is a survival mechanism. For self-preservation, the primitive parts of our brains are wired to separate friends from foes. However, in today's modern world with major improvements in medicine, education, technology and food production, these primitive survival skills are no longer necessary.

What worked for our ancestral hunter-gatherers doesn't always work for us now. For instance, our ancestral human instinct tells our body to consume sugar and fat because in earlier times we did not know when or where the next meal would come. Today most people can just go to the store and buy their next meal; therefore, our human body does not need to store up sugar and fat. Today we do not need to feel in danger of being attacked by those who seem to be different; they are not enemies and are not dangerous. We can now start to not hate other people. *"I will not hate you."*

We are taught to hate the enemy, and the enemy is anyone who is different from us. This leaves little room for vulnerability and a chance to explore the empathy of other people. Our family history, our culture and our political history of today are highly competitive and promote a culture of violence.

To hate is becoming more normal and socially acceptable. Those who think differently become enemies, and many political leaders promote this. Just look at what various political leaders promote in countries such as the USA, China and Russia. There is great hatred and division in many countries, especially amongst political parties.

Daily we see and hear hatred on social media, the news, social media groups and many other places, to the point that hate has taken over our emotions. We may have become emotionally incompetent, and that's why we hate others. When we do not call out the immoral conduct of these leaders and take sides with them, then we are not only legitimizing their attacks and divisive behaviors but also fueling hate. *"I will not hate you."*

Sometimes people hate because they themselves are insecure. They compare themselves to other people, and when they conclude the other person is better than they are and possess traits they do not have, they dislike or hate the other person. Sometimes people hate because they have low self-esteem; it feels better for them to express their negativity by blaming someone else rather than to confront their own problems. Sometimes people hate because they have high anxiety, and they project their anxiety onto other people. Sometimes we fear ourselves, claiming, "I am not terrible, you are the one who is terrible," when actually we need to change ourselves in order to love ourselves, so that we can love others as we love ourselves.

When we find parts of ourselves unacceptable, we go on to attack others in order to defend against those threats. Therefore, if we have a lot of hate for another person, then we will have a lot of hate for ourselves. We have to learn to love ourselves, so that we can love others as we love ourselves. If you don't like what you see in the mirror, then make the necessary changes in your life.

Highly successful, popular and generous people attract hatred because people are envious and jealous of them. Sometimes people draw hate to themselves because they are full of envy, gluttony, greed, lust, pride, laziness and anger. Sometimes people are hated because they are pompous, narcissistic, self-centered, self-serving, rude, quick-tempered, never accountable, always blaming others, rejoicing over others' misfortunes and other undesirable traits. It does not matter what undesirable traits the other person has; it is your goal to not hate that person. You are responsible for your morality, your soul and your efforts to avoid hell. *"I will not hate you."*

In 1984 when I attended Embry Riddle Aeronautical University, I rented a house with two friends, Doug and Don. I liked both my housemates, but there was a time when I hated Doug. Doug and I were enrolled in the same college course, "Advanced Aerodynamics II." That year I enrolled in 54 college credit hours including four flight courses; I had taken on a full plate of college studies.

"Advanced Aerodynamics II" was a really tough class, and I had to study night and day just to get a C grade. That lowered my GPA to 3.1, and I was not happy. However, Doug would only have to see, hear, or read the course material and formulas once and he knew the material. He barely studied for any exams, and yet he obtained a B grade. I was jealous and envious of him. Maybe I didn't really hate him, but I surely didn't like him during that semester.

Why did I have to study so hard and he barely spent any time studying, and yet he obtained a B grade while I obtained a C grade? That wasn't fair. Eventually I learned that Doug had a photographic memory. He had previously been in the United States Air Force and had been tasked with listening to Russian intelligence and converting that information into an encrypted code that would be forwarded onto the highest level of US military intelligence.

Doug had the ability to remember information and visual images in great detail. Once I fully comprehended and accepted this special skill of Doug's, I forgave him. Soon thereafter I rightfully forgave myself for disliking my friend just because he had skills I did not have. I forgave myself for being jealous and envious of Doug's skills. God gave him certain skills, and God gave me other skills. I chose to accept this and move on.

CHAPTER NINE

NOT HATE FOR HEALTH

There are several reasons why we should not hate. For the good of people and the planet, we should not hate. Not hating helps us avoid hell. By not hating others, we can avoid bad feelings, a guilty conscience and other detrimental emotions. There are also health consequences such as stress when we hate. There are health benefits such as the release of endorphins when we do not hate and when we like instead.

When we hate someone, there are health consequences such as the effects of stress on the human body. Stress can be really bad for you. Hating someone creates negative feelings that put stress on our bodies. Distress (bad stress), can seriously damage performance and can lead to serious physical and mental illness if not controlled.

The long-term effects of distress can cause physical and psychological symptoms such as gastrointestinal problems (diarrhea or nausea), depression or severe headaches. Other long-term effects of distress are insomnia and heart disease, and developing bad habits (such as drinking, overeating, smoking and using drugs to cope). Other negative long-term effects stress can lead to are feelings of distrust, rejection, anger and depression, which can lead to health problems such as headaches, upset stomach, rashes, insomnia, ulcers, high blood pressure, heart disease and stroke.

Long-term stress is best managed by changes to lifestyle, attitude and environment. Maintain your emotional reserves. Develop mutually supportive friends and relationships.

Learn to not hate people. Your health may depend on it. Search and discover one personal trait in a person that will help you not hate them and maybe like them and eventually love them. *"I will not hate you."*

There are health benefits to not hating someone and liking or helping someone. When you help a person feel good, your emotions of self-satisfaction increase your level of endorphins, which kick in when we receive satisfaction. Endorphins are chemicals produced by the body that reduce pain and boost pleasure, resulting in a feeling of euphoria. They work similarly to opioid drugs, as when morphine is prescribed for short-term use after surgery to reduce pain. Endorphins produce positive feelings in the body, similar to morphine.

People who do physical workouts or who run experience this positive feeling of well-being due to the rise in endorphins. Sometimes, I force myself to go for a swim, but I do so knowing how great I will feel afterwards, when the endorphins kick in. When you exercise, your body releases endorphin chemicals that trigger positive feelings in the body and reduce your perception of pain. It's like taking morphine without the damage. I feel great after exercising, especially after a swim, because of endorphins. Loving someone and helping someone produce similar effects to getting morphine, but without the addictive side effects.

One of the ways to not hate someone is to smile at that person and try to communicate with them. There are health benefits to communicating and socializing.

Socializing may improve your physical health and your mental health.

It may improve your brain's health and lower your risk of dementia. Socializing may help fight off depression. Positive social bonds may help build a stronger immune system. People with more social support tend to live longer than those who are isolated.

Socializing is also fun. Helping others may improve your health and extend your lifespan. The more you socialize with a person the more chance there is that you will not hate that person and that you will start liking that person. "I will not hate you."

CHAPTER TEN

How to Not Hate

One way to start to not hate someone is to find a healthy way to communicate with that person. Look that person in the eyes, give them a big, happy smile and say something nice to that person, like "you have a nice smile."

When starting up a conversation, sidestep issues that affect you emotionally. Instead of reacting or overreacting, make a statement showing that you understand how the other person feels and showing how you feel. Be mindful of your emotions. Avoid confrontation and limit your conversation to the issues you're comfortable with. Stay composed and give yourself emotional space if you feel the conversation is becoming difficult. Don't let the other person affect your emotions in a negative way.

Put a positive spin on how you perceive that person, and avoid any negative assumptions you have about them. Instead of fixating on how much you dislike a person, focus on your strategy on how you will improve your feelings about that person. You only have control of yourself and your actions, so don't let that person drag you down and influence you to hate them. *"I will not hate you."*

What do you have in common with that person? Spend more time with that person and find some common ground. I have been amazed how often I have found something in common with a person I thought was a complete opposite of me. Taking the time to understand the person you hate can help you have more empathy and compassion for them. By building rapport with them, you can start not hating them and be on your way to liking them.

Avoid and ignore personal attacks. Take a deep breath, quiet your mind, listen more, talk less and let them go. Be self-confident and secure with who you are in order to not let what others say about you bother you. Don't let the other person affect your emotions in a negative way. Acquire the attitude, "Frankly my dear, I don't give a damn," as spoken by Rhett Butler to Scarlett in the movie *Gone with the Wind*.

Piloting jets can be very stressful at times, with changing work schedules, emergencies and a whole slew of events that could happen: maintenance issues, weather problems, air traffic delays, physical or mental fatigue, medical exams, flight check rides, training, et cetera. While piloting a jet airplane, your body is operating at a heightened state of physical and mental alertness, especially during challenging landings. Imagine this for a challenging landing: very strong crosswinds; a slippery, snowy runway during minimum low visibility; a short distance runway; maximum jet airplane landing weight; the end of a long demanding flight duty day. To alleviate the adrenaline rush from landing a wide-body jet or, sometimes just to relax, I practice meditation.

Meditation reduces stress, anxiety and aggression. Daily meditation helps to reinforce and integrate your body's rhythms. There are many benefits of meditation.

First, it can help most people relax and feel less anxious and more in control. It also increases self-confidence and feelings of connection to others. It increases self-actualization, emotional stability, happiness and feelings of vitality and rejuvenation. It helps decrease depression, irritability and moodiness. It promotes harmony of brainwave activity in different parts of the brain and is associated with greater creativity, improved moral reasoning and higher IQ. It can help improve learning ability and memory.

Meditation can help you to not hate. Start meditating to help improve your mental and physical health; that will help you on your path to not hate a particular person or persons. While meditating, you can home in on the phrase *"I will not hate you."* Breathe in and say or think, *"I will not hate you."* Breathe out and say or think, *"I will not hate you."*

Be a good neighbor and treat everyone with politeness, courtesy and respect, even when you disagree. Put on your best manners and treat others as you would like to be treated by others.

Over my thirty-year career as an airline pilot I have flown with over one thousand pilots, pilots who may differ from me in ethnicity, religion, social class, social groups, culture, cuisine preference, social habits, musical taste, values, et cetera. I would meet the other pilot for the pre-flight crew brief, a man or a woman from any background from anywhere in the USA, and one hour later we were safely operating a jet as a team from departure airport to destination airport. Sometimes we were flying together as a flight crew for the first time on an eight-hour flight across the ocean to a foreign country, and the crew was together for a ten-day flight trip. Meet a co-worker for the first time and work together for a day or ten days—I am unaware of any other profession on planet Earth that operates like this.

One time I met my copilot at 1:00 a.m. in the hotel lobby to fly a seven-day trip together. This quiet guy was from Texas and spoke with a strong, slow Southern accent; I, who am from Long Island, was so different from him in every way. My first impression was, how am I ever going to get along with this person for seven days?

But don't judge a book by its cover; read at least the first chapter. (By the way, thank you for getting this far reading my words). Don't let the first impression that the other person is so different from you dictate how you will get along. We discovered things we had in common, such as that we had a similar comedian sense of humor. Excluding those first few hours, we got along great during the entire seven-day flight trip. I had to accept that person and quickly gel as a team; the safety of the flight depended on it.

Some may wonder what I mean when I say the safety of flight depended on it. First, we must understand that it takes two pilots to operate a sophisticated jet airplane. During normal operations, one pilot (the flying pilot) flies the jet, and the other pilot (the non-flying pilot) navigates the jet and communicates with Air Traffic Control. Each pilot has other duties that they perform as well.

If an emergency or an abnormal situation should occur, it becomes more crucial to work as a team and trust each other. During an emergency, like the 2009 "Miracle on the Hudson" emergency with Sully Sullenberger, saving lives depends on working as a team and trusting each other.

Generally, during an emergency, one pilot flies the plane, navigates and communicates, while the other pilot executes and completes all normal and emergency checklist procedures. The cockpit duties are split up, and each pilot is working in his or her own world during the emergency. Each pilot must put great trust in the other pilot.

The flying pilot will update the non-flying pilot on the progress of the flight. The non-flying pilot will update the flying pilot on the aircraft conditions and the requirements and progress of all checklists that will need to be completed. The pilots will rejoin as a team before landing.

The pilots must work as a team and must trust each other. Survival of life is much more important than the reasons why you don't like the other person. There is no time to hate or dislike your coworker; the safety of the flight depends on it.

Instead of judging others, judge yourself. Did you ever think maybe they hate you? Are you full of envy, gluttony, greed, lust, pride, laziness and anger? Are you jealous, envious or resentful of the person you hate?

Look at yourself; maybe you share some of the blame. Maybe you need to make changes in your life that will help them not hate you. Recognize the value in different opinions and understand other people's perspectives. See their side. Put yourself in their shoes and try to see how others perceive you.

Seek a support system, a circle of trusted friends, a mentor or a trusted colleague to help you on a path to how to not hate a particular person. Sometimes just knowing that another person understands what you're going through can be helpful, and they may provide a new perspective on how to stop hating that person. Seek help and pray. Even Jesus prayed for help, and even Jesus needed help carrying His cross.

We can look upon Jesus as the ultimate example of how not to hate. Jesus fed the hungry, healed the sick, forgave sinners' sins, wept for mourners and loved all people. Not only did Jesus display sorrow, sympathy and compassion for all mankind, but He also forgave everyone for their wrongdoings.

During one of Jesus's most frightful times, the time when He was praying in the Garden of Olives, His friends could not even stay awake to support and comfort Him.

One of Jesus's friends, Judas, betrayed Him by arranging for soldiers to arrest Him. After He was arrested, all of His friends deserted Him. One of Jesus's best friends, Peter, three times denied knowing Him when Peter's loyalty to Jesus was tested.

Jesus was stripped of His clothes and brutally tortured. A crown of spiky thorns was inserted onto His head, puncturing the skin in many places, while others struck Him and called Him names. While His body was in total despair from physical punishment, He was made to carry a heavy wooden cross for approximately three-quarters of a mile. Soldiers pounded nails into Jesus's hands and feet and hung Him on a cross. The chief priest and others mocked Him while He was drastically suffering on the cross, a suffering that may have lasted over six hours. When Jesus moaned of being thirsty, they offered Him sour wine vinegar.

Any one of these actions would have provided justification for hating those persons. And what did Jesus do and say? **"Father, forgive them, they know not what they do"** (Luke 23:34). Jesus forgave all of them—His enemies and His friends. Not only did Jesus forgive one of His best friends, Peter, He also arranged for Peter to be the leader of the new Christian religion. O dear Jesus, for the sake of Your sorrowful passion, have mercy on us and on the whole world and help us to not hate. *"I will not hate you."*

Okay, I get it—we are not Jesus, and we may never be as strong as He was at forgiving and not hating. Chade-Meng Tan, a former mindfulness pioneer at Google and the author of *Search Inside Yourself,* teaches a brilliant and highly effective "kindness-mindful" exercise. Here is my variation of the "kindness-mindful" exercise with a technique consisting of four steps you can practice to help you not hate a person.

Step one: Wish happiness and love onto yourself. Experience these euphoric feelings. Obtaining happiness and love is a matter of perspective and will vary for each individual. Some will wish for a close relationship, marriage, Holy Orders, becoming a parent, helping others or performing a simple act of kindness. Others will wish for a promotion, money, material goods, good health, a good night's sleep or maybe just food and water for the day.

For this technique, I will wish for a grand, fantastic party, a party for me. In this imaginary wish, everyone I know and many more people that I do not know are attending this event just for me. Each person is there to love, to honor and to glorify me. Each person presents to me a totally satisfying gift.

I am the most popular person at this grand party. I am so happy; everyone is there for me, and everyone is loving and honoring me. At this party there are the best special foods and drinks, videos, music, games, dancing, singing, praying, laughing, holding hands, hugging, kissing, magic tricks, comedians, guest speakers, toasting and compliments galore for the guest of honor of the party: me. I absorb and consume this experience of euphoric feelings. I am so happy and I feel so loved.

Step two: Choose a person, such as a loved one or a good friend, a person who is easy to love or not hate, and wish these same feelings of happiness and love onto that person. I wish that my wife, or son, or daughter, or mother, or father, or brother, or sister, or best friend would be given a fantastic party. I wish that this person will experience the same euphoric feeling of happiness and love that I experienced. Everyone they know and many more people that they do not know will attend the party.

Each person is there to just love, honor and glorify him or her. The guest of honor will receive fantastic gifts from those who attend. The grand party will have a great ambiance and the best entertainment, all customized for this person, the person you love, who will be the most popular person at this grand party. This person will be very happy and feel very loved, knowing that everyone is there for them to love, to honor and to glorify them.

Step three: Select some neutral person whom you don't have any strong feelings for or against and wish happiness and love onto that person. I do not personally know our mailman, but I wish there would be a great fantastic party held for him. Everything that I imagined in my party would be at the party for the mailman. He is the most popular person at this grand party. The mailman is so happy that everyone is there just for him, and everyone is there to love, honor and glorify him.

Step four, the final step: Take this same wish of happiness and love and project these feelings toward the person you hate. I do not like Lucifer—in fact I hate Lucifer—but I wish happiness and love onto Lucifer. I wish there would be a great fantastic party held for Lucifer. Everyone that Lucifer knows and many more people that he does not know will attend this party. Everything I envisioned at my imaginary party would be at Lucifer's party.

Each person will be there to love, honor and glorify Lucifer. Each person will present a special great gift to him. He is the most popular person at this grand party. Lucifer is so happy that everyone is there just for him and everyone is there to love, honor and glorify him.

The last step in this exercise may not be easy to accomplish. You may have to practice the previous steps of this technique several times before you are able to successfully implement the final step of not to hate that person in question. Meditate and project good feelings toward the person you're endeavoring not to hate. Love yourself, love another loved person, love a neutral bystander and eventually love the one you hate.

Success can be obtained by accomplishing step-by-step achievements toward this endeavor. First, try not to hate the one you hate, then try to like that person and eventually love that person and every person as much as you love yourself. Monitor the progress of your capacity to love all humans on planet Earth. *"I will not hate you."*

You may need a grace blessing to help you not hate a certain person. Grace is the unconditional gift of love toward a person who may not deserve it. Grace is the help that God gives us to strengthen our relationship with God and other people. There is sanctifying grace that stays in the soul and makes the soul holy; there is actual grace that encourages the soul to be more holy and loving.

With a grace blessing you are asking for the spiritual influence to operate within you to strengthen your love. A blessing is a special favor, mercy, praise, devotion or worship, such as the grace blessing prayed before a meal. "Bless us, O Lord, and these thy gifts which we are about to receive from thy bounty, through Christ, Our Lord, Amen." At the end of this chapter is my "Grace Blessing," a prayer to Mary requesting grace for another person.

There are many Christian faith traditions. Although most Christians believe Mary is the mother of Jesus Christ, some believe Mary must not get in the way of their personal relationship with Jesus and their personal acceptance of Jesus as their Lord and Savior. Some believe that Mary has no role in the larger work of God's salvation through Jesus.

However, I believe that Mary can be a so-called middleman or "middlewoman" between Jesus and us. Mary is the mother of Jesus, and Jesus, like most children, desires to please his mother. Having a good personal relationship with Mary, the mother of Jesus, will help you improve your relationship with Mary's son, Jesus.

When there was a wine shortage at the wedding in Cana in Galilee, Mary made a request to her son to help solve the wine problem. Are you not more important than the lack of wine at a wedding? Pray, beg and plead to Mary to make a request to Jesus on your behalf for help—help to not hate.

I read one time that Holy Mary, the mother of God, revealed that she had many grace blessings to offer, more than the number of requests for her blessings. I tried to find the citation to give credit to the writer, but I could not find the source. But that statement is implanted in my brain's bank of memories.

Mary has many grace blessings to grant—blessings just waiting for our request. You can request this grace blessing for anyone: someone you know or someone you don't know, someone you like or someone you don't like, someone you love or do not love, or someone you may hate. It would be nice if you could put your hand on the person's forehead while saying the grace blessing for them, but it is not necessary.

If there's a person you dislike and that person is aggravating you, just say the grace blessing for them. Shoot the grace blessing prayer at them. Imagine you are shooting a prayer laser to them. Sometimes when that person is yelling at you, or disgusting you and testing your self-control, just look that person in the eyes and say the grace blessing.

Here is the prayer I call the "Grace Blessing prayer." This is a tool I use to give a grace blessing to someone. If you are able and have the person's permission, put your hand on the person's forehead—for example, say the person's name is Veronica—and say, "Hail Mary full of grace, open up your hands and shine a ray of grace onto

Veronica." The appendix includes a copy of this prayer for you to use. You can use this prayer and customize the name for your situation.

CHAPTER ELEVEN

Start Now to Not Hate

If you deduce that you are making progress in not hating a person or people and are moving up the ladder of liking or maybe even loving, then take not hating someone to the next level and embrace philanthropy. A philanthropist helps people in need by giving time, money and/or gifts to charities. Helping others will make you feel good by doing something good for the good of people and planet Earth. Giving gives you a sense of renewal, enables you to feel thankful, and may help you find your inner peace. Giving can boost your self-esteem and provide a sense of belonging. Giving may help save lives by just providing a meal to someone starving. Volunteering improves your ability to manage stress, helps reduce rates of depression, alleviates loneliness and increases a sense of life satisfaction. These are some of the factors that can significantly benefit our long-term health.

One option is to donate to a charity relief service. One of the charities I donate to is a humanitarian charity started in 1943 that is dedicated to helping the world's poor. It has a four-star rating, and 93 percent of the charity's total expenses are spent on the programs and services it delivers.

Another charitable organization I donate to has been in existence for over 75 years, is the fifth-largest charity in the US, and is dedicated to reducing poverty in America. It has a four-star rating, and 93 percent of the charity's total expenses are spent on the programs and services it delivers. This organization has local chapters scattered throughout the USA.

Donate to your local church, synagogue, mosque or community. Every charitable organization is in need of funds. At Christmas time, many churches today have a giving tree.

Cards used as ornaments are hung on a Christmas tree. The cards are encrypted with a specific gift request such as "age 9—boy, size 8 shoes" or "age 6—girl, size small winter coat," et cetera. Pick a card, purchase the gift, wrap the gift with an appropriate gift card and return it to the giving tree. The gifts are placed under the tree and eventually distributed just before Christmas Day. There are no names on the card; the giver is anonymous to the receiver.

For those with scarce funds to donate, you can donate your time. I help with the Social ministries of our church, particularly the Judea Christian Outreach Center. Through this service, we purchase food, prepare meals and serve the meals to those who are hungry and in need of food. We cook up a ham and potato gratin casserole and serve it with salad, beans, fruit, rolls, desserts, iced tea, milk and water. On Wednesdays I deliver meals for the food bank to those in need. It is so satisfying serving a meal to a hungry person, especially when that person looks you in the eye and expresses a truthful thank you.

Another generous person and I co-run and organize six garden vegetable plots for our church. We cultivate, plant, weed, water and harvest vegetables. On the last Saturday of every month, our church donates food, toiletries and clothes to the needy. We harvest the crops from this vegetable garden to add to the food pantry for the monthly distribution.

With six other adults and eight teen leaders, I help teach religion to teenagers. Ironically, there are many occasions when the teens are teaching me.

There is always a need for blood, so several times a year I give a double red cell donation, which is two units of red blood cells. Giving blood helps someone else and also helps you with certain health benefits.

Whenever I am traveling, I offer help to a local church while on layover. I have never been turned down. There is always a need for human labor to help with something.

My previous book, the Ten Healthy Tips (click), was another way for me to give back to humanity. That book takes readers into the mind of an airline pilot and the health tips he practiced throughout his airline career. That book provided a flight plan to help you enhance your well-being and improve your mental and physical health. I figured that if just one healthy tip helped just one person in some way, then I am happily rewarded that I have given back to help mankind.

I do not want to sound braggadocious because my efforts are minuscule compared to what Jesus has done for us. These are just a few ideas of what I am doing to not hate people. This is my way of cleaning up or lighting up my soul, my scorecard, so that on that day when I die, God will not send me to hell—maybe purgatory, and hopefully heaven, but not to hell.

Save us from the fires of hell. Maybe there is a hell, and if you grow in a personal way to like or love all people, then maybe you could avoid going to hell. This book is about not hating other people. But what right do I have to write about not to hate? After all I am not the Pope, Muhammad, the Dalai Lama, the Grand Ayatollah, Sri Mata, Yona

Metzger, the Archbishop of Canterbury, or any significant holy leader. I have no credentials. I am just one earthly human being trying to clean up my soul and maybe help you, too. I am trying to give back, and I believe the Holy Spirit influenced me to write this for you.

Helping people and or doing something for someone may create the greatest reward and satisfaction for both giver and receiver. Giving and helping others may be the greatest therapy to longevity and happiness.

Start now, because you never know when life will end. Life is precious, delicate and unpredictable. Start now not to hate. Start at home. Do not hate anyone at home.

Begin with the "grace blessing prayer" on your family and friends. Expand your circle of humans you do not want to hate. Do not hate here, there or anywhere. Do not hate yourself, anyone or me.

Remember you have to love yourself before you can love others as yourself. If you look in the mirror and do not like what you see, then make the necessary changes in your life. Do not hate lovers, friends and enemies. Do not hate today, tomorrow and every day in the future. Use the "Trinity for Me" prayer to be thankful for your progress in not hating and to request help to not hate anyone, anywhere, anytime. Love or like other humans, but DO NOT hate them or anyone.

All of us are capable of looking at another person, giving them a big smile and shooting up a prayer for them. Sometimes just looking at a person in the eye and giving them a big smile is the hardest thing to do, but it is a great start to *"I will not hate you."*

Who are we? Why were we created? Why are we here? What is our purpose in this life? Are we here to just suck everything we can out of people and Earth's resources?

Or should we give back to the people and planet Earth? Should we pray for people? Should we make sacrifices for people? Should we help and love people? Should we like people? Should we hate people?

The genetic DNA makeup of all humans is 99.9 percent identical. All of us humans are equal and will be judged by some type of non-human scorecard by God. God made you and God made me. I have no idea how He will judge you and me on His non-human terms. The best I can do is to ignore your faults and highlight your virtues and try to love you—or at least not hate you.

We all have a chance for heaven or hell. You don't have to be old to not hate and you don't have to be an adult to not hate. **No matter where you are and where you have been, you can start not hating.** Everyone is capable of not hating.

Let's start on a path to heaven by not hating any human. **I WILL NOT HATE YOU.** I will try to like you. I will try to love you, but I **WILL NOT HATE YOU**. If just one tip or suggestion from this book influences just one person in some way Not to Hate one person, then I am happily rewarded and my revised lifelong goal to help mankind has been achieved.

"I will not hate you."

Acknowledgments

I would like to thank Lauren Tompkins for her prompt and professional proofreading service. Thank you, Paraclete Multimedia for your valuable contributions. I thank Adrian, Dane and John Low of Ebook Launch for their expertise in book design and book formatting. Thank you, Doctor Ted Kubicki, for your spiritual influence and for writing the Foreword. I thank all the people I have associated with through the various charitable and philanthropic groups I am involved in. A particular thank you to the Holy Family Life teen group for the positive religious influence you have had on me. I thank the Holy Spirit for inspiring and guiding me to write this book. I thank my mother and father for giving birth to me and raising me, and I thank my loving wife and God for giving me the precious opportunity to be a husband and father. To my sons, who have motivated me to write this book, I wish the best of all good things to come to you in this earthly life and in the life to come. God bless.

APPENDIX

TRINITY FOR ME

O my dear God
O my dear Jesus
And the Holy Spirit,
Thank You for this moment of life.
Thank You for this breath of air.
Thank You for providing water and food for my body,
And thank You for protecting, guiding, and nourishing my soul.
Thank You for _____.
Please help and/or grant me with _____.
Please protect and guide my thoughts, words, heart, and soul
Toward you during this earthly journey so that after this life I will be in heaven.
Please help me to love God, myself, and everyone.
I love you, trust you, believe in you, and hope to be with you.
Amen.

GRACE BLESSING

Hail Mary full of grace, open up your hands and shine a ray of grace onto _____

Bibliography

1. Fellows, Mark. E. Sister Lucia Apostle of Mary's Immaculate Hearth. Buffalo: Immaculate Heart Publications, 2007. 227

2. http://fatima.org/wp-content/uploads/2018/05/sister-Lucy-sm.pdf (accessed April 17, 2020)

3. Davies, Paul. The Accidental Universe. Cambridge: Cambridge University Press. 1982. 118

4. Davies, Paul. Superforce: The Search for the Grand Unified Theory of Nature. New York: Simon and Schuster, 194. 242

5. Hawking, Stephen. A Brief History of Time. New York: Bantam Books, 1996. 126.

6. Bradley, Walter L. The Say So Universe, in Signs of Intelligence. Grand Rapid, MI: Brazos Press, 2001. 169

7. Penrose, Roger. The Emperor's New Mind. New York: Oxford, 1989. 344

8. Davies, Paul. Cosmic Jackpot. New York: Houghton Mifflin, 2007. 149

9 Dawkins, Richard. The God Delusion. New York: Marinet Books, 2008. 258

10. "Web Bible," Christian Answers. 1998-2013. Http://christiananswers.net/ bible/home.html (accessed April 4, 2012)

11. Christian Violotti, http://ancient.cu/Jesus_Christ.html (accessed April 3, 2020)

12. Ibid.

13. "Major Religions of the World Ranked by Numbers of Adherents," Adherents. Last modified August 9, 2007. http://www.adherents.com/Religions_By _ Adherents.html

14. Clemmons, Nancy. Exploring the Religions of Our World. Notre Dame: Ave Maria Press, Inc., 2008. 292

15. Ibid. 334

16. Peters, F.E. "Abraham's Miraculous Journey," U.S. News and World Report, March 13, 2007. 18

17. "Jewish Virtual Library," The American-Israel Cooperative Enterprise.2012. http://jewishvirtuallibrary.org/jsources/glossT.html (accessed April 5, 2012)

18. Ibid.

19. Holy Bible, the New American Bible. Nashville: Thomas Nelson, Inc. 1998.

20. "Crash Course Series on Introductory Judaism," Hanefesh. 2011. http://hanefesh.com/Crash_Course.html

21. "Web Bible," Christian Answers. 1998-2013. Http://christiananswers.net/ bible/home.html (accessed April 4, 2012)

22-25. Francis, James Allan. The Real Jesus and Other Sermons. Philadelphia: Judson Press, 1926. 121

26. "The Profession of Faith, Catechism of the Catholic Faith," Vatican.2005

http://vactican.va/archive/ccc_css/archive/catechism/credo.html (accessed March 14, 2013)

27. "The Our Father, Catechism of the Catholic Faith," Ibid.

28. Peterson, Eugene. The Message//Remix. Colorado Springs: Navpress Publishing Group, 2003. 1775

29. Catholic Prayer for Catholic Families. Chicago: Loyola Press, 2006.

30. Clemmons, Nancy. Exploring the Religions of Our World. Notre Dame: Ave Maria Press, Inc., 2008. 320

Notes

[1] Mark E. Fellows, *Sister Lucia: Apostle of Mary's Immaculate Heart* (Buffalo, NY: Immaculate Heart Publications, 2007), 227.

[2] http://fatima.org/wp-content/uploads/2018/05/sister-Lucy-sm.pdf.

[3] Paul Davies, *The Accidental Universe* (Cambridge: Cambridge University Press, 1982), 118.

[4] Paul Davies, *Superforce: The Search for the Grand Unified Theory of Nature* (New York: Simon and Schuster, 194), 242.

[5] Stephen Hawking, *A Brief History of Time* (New York: Bantam Books, 1996), 126.

[6] Walter L. Bradley, "The Say So Universe," in *Signs of Intelligence* (Grand Rapid, MI: Brazos, 2001), 169.

[7] Roger Penrose, *The Emperor's New Mind* (New York: Oxford, 1989), 344.

[8] Paul Davies, *Cosmic Jackpot* (New York: Houghton Mifflin, 2007), 149.

[9] Richard Dawkins, *The God Delusion* (New York: Marinet, 2008), 258.

[10] "Web Bible," Christian Answers. 1998-2013. http://christiananswers.net/ bible/home.html.

[11] Christian Violotti, http://ancient.cu/Jesus_Christ.html.

[12] Ibid.

13 "Major Religions of the World Ranked by Numbers of Adherents," http://www.adherents.com/Religions_By_Adherents.html

14 Nancy Clemmons, *Exploring the Religions of Our World* (Notre Dame, IN: Ave Maria Press, 2008) 292.

15 Clemmons, *Exploring the Religions of Our World*, 334.

16 F. E. Peters, "Abraham's Miraculous Journey," *U.S. News and World Report*, March 13, 2007, 18.

17 "Jewish Virtual Library," The American-Israel Cooperative Enterprise, http://jewishvirtuallibrary.org/jsources/glossT.html.

18 Ibid.

19 *Holy Bible, the New American Bible* (Nashville, TN: Thomas Nelson, 2020).

20 "Crash Course Series on Introductory Judaism," http://hanefesh.com/Crash_Course.html.

21 "Web Bible," Christian Answers. 1998-2013, http://christiananswers.net/ bible/home.html.

22 James Allan Francis, *The Real Jesus and Other Sermons* (Philadelphia: Judson Press, 1926), 121.

23 Ibid.

24 Ibid.

25 Ibid.

26 "The Profession of Faith, Catechism of the Catholic Faith," http://vatican.va/archive/ccc_css/archive/catechism/credo.html.

[27] "The Our Father, Catechism of the Catholic Faith,". http://vatican.va/archive/ccc_css/archive/catechism/credo.html.

[28] Eugene Peterson. *The Message//Remix* (Colorado Springs, CO: Navpress, 2003), 1775.

[29] *Catholic Prayer for Catholic Families*. Chicago: Loyola Press, 2006.

[30] Clemmons, *Exploring the Religions of Our World*, 320.

About the Author

Frank J Donohue, born in New York in 1961, is an American pilot, author and video producer. Frank served four years in the United States Air Force from 1979 to 1981. During that time, Frank obtained an associate's degree in resource management and a private pilot license. He graduated with a bachelor's degree in Aeronautical Science from Embry Riddle Aeronautical University in 1985. After various pilot jobs, Frank methodically worked his way up the ranks to a pilot position with Flying Tigers in 1987. FedEx and Flying Tigers merged in 1989. Frank flew for FedEx for over 30 years and retired in 2017. Frank authored the books "School and Schooled" in 2014 and "Ten Healthy Tips" in 2019, "From Hate to Love" in 2020 and produced pilot videos in 2019. Frank and his wife live in Virginia Beach but continue to travel. They have two grown children. Frank has volunteered coaching basketball, soccer, and baseball. Currently he is a Life Teen leader, teaching religion at his local church to teenagers. He is a supporter of a variety of philanthropic organizations.

Author's Note

From Hate to Love: A Spiritual Journey to Heal was written, designed, produced and published by its author. It is really hard to put a good book together. I invite you to post an honest and objective review of this book in the online bookstore of your choice. Your comments will help improve the quality of what good writers write and what good readers read. Thank you for reading my words.

https://frankjdonohue.com/

https://not-y.com/

www.ingramcontent.com/pod-product-compliance
Lightning Source LLC
Chambersburg PA
CBHW072100290426
44110CB00014B/1764